MW01594967

THE GAME
OF WEALTH

*A Strategy for Winning Wealth
and Living a Full Life*

THE GAME
OF WEALTH

*A Strategy for Winning Wealth
and Living a Full Life*

*May all your
Dreams be realized*

Co-Authored By

Ray Haskell & Reg Redding

ΛWΛ

Affiliated Writers of America / Casa Grande, Arizona
Imprint of Alexander & Hayes Publishing, Inc.

Copyright 2009 by Ray Haskell and Reg Redding. All rights reserved, including the right to reproduce this book or portions thereof in any form without written permission from the publisher.

ISBN: 978-1-879915-21-3

Library of Congress Control Number: 2009933232

Published by Affiliated Writers of America
An Imprint of Alexander & Hayes Publishing, Inc.
P.O. Box 11107
Casa Grande, Arizona 85230
480-430-4339

Cover Art, Cover Illustration(s), and Cover Design Copyright 2009 by Alexander & Hayes Publishing, Inc.
Cover Design, Book Design, Typesetting, and Computer Graphics by Jayme Fraser

Scripture taken from the HOLY BIBLE, NEW INTERNATIONAL VERSION ®. Copyright © 1973, 1978, 1984 by International Bible Society. Used by permission of Zondervan Publishing House. All rights reserved.

Manufactured in the United States of America

TABLE OF CONTENTS

ACKNOWLEDGEMENTS

Ray Haskell

Thanks to all of those who have influenced me to live life to the fullest at the same time reminding me to take the time and enjoy the journey along the way. I would like to give special thanks to:

My lovely wife, Sheila, who has provided the silent unwavering support by believing in me and walking side-by-side, hand-in-hand along the journey of life. I love her with all my heart.

My children, Andrew and Amy, who are the most inspirational individuals anyone could ever meet. Andrew by, from the outset of putting this book together, stating, "It is easier said than done." Amy, who from her competitive spirit, drives me forward reminding me that success can be derived from anything that we do, not just contests we find ourselves in.

My father, Richard Haskell, and my sisters Rinda, Jennifer, Tomie and Jacqueline, who have all in their own ways spurred me on to be the best that I can be no matter what the circumstance.

Jay Carswell, who early in my working career perhaps even unknowingly put me in my place by reminding me what life is really about by clearly defining what "wealth" is.

Jay Fraser and Reg Redding, partners and friends who have provided the support, inspiration, motivation and laughs in sharing their knowledge and experiences that have gone into this project. Truly, thank you and may all the joys of life be yours along the way.

Reg Redding

Special thanks to:

My Mother—for loving me and believing in me. She was an angel.

My Dad—for being himself and standing up for his ways, even though many times I disagreed with him.

My two sisters, Kay and Sheila—for always being there and for not being alike—always giving me two ways to look at things, and a totally different conversation.

My long-term buddy Ron Anderson—always a rock, always there. For giving me great advice and encouragement. For teaching me about the joy of giving. A top friend who loves me just for who I am.

My pal Ray Haskell—for caring, listening, sharing, mentoring, tolerating me, and for our special friendship.

My long-term friend Kay Palmer—no one can equal her friendship and loyalty.

And most importantly, thanks to God for life, countless blessings, for bringing me through trials, the gift of salvation, and for the special people above. I am blessed.

About the Authors

Raymond Haskell currently resides in the Wichita, Kansas area with his wife Sheila, whom he met while attending the University of Oklahoma, and two children—Andrew and Amy. He was born in southeastern Colorado in the small town of Lamar, where he was the second of five children, having one older and three younger sisters.

He attended the University of Denver studying economics and accounting directly out of high school. He graduated from the University of Oklahoma in 1991 with a Bachelors of Accountancy Degree with a second major in Finance.

He obtained Securities and Insurance Licenses in 1993 and has worked in the field of accounting and finance for public and private companies over the last 18 years. He has also worked part time over the past 15 years doing financial analysis for individuals in preparing risk management (insurance) and investment strategies.

Reg Redding resides in Wichita, Kansas and has been a licensed Certified Public Accountant for more than 25 years. He earned his Bachelor of Science Degree in Accounting from Emporia State University in Emporia, Kansas and began his career working for a CPA firm for nearly five years. He is currently employed as a corporate payroll and benefits manager.

He is a long-term member of the Institute of Management Accountants and serves on the Board of Directors for the Wichita, Kansas chapter. He was raised on a ranch in the Flint Hills region of east-central Kansas, and enjoys spending time with family, gardening, antiquing, playing piano, and collecting classic automobiles.

Co-Authors

We have written this book as a couple of friends who had kicked around the idea for several years. It is our goal that you will learn something from our ideas, thoughts, suggestions, and tips and can put those to good use in making your life more enjoyable. In these writings, there are many stories that obviously relate to only one of us, as both of us have different relatives, backgrounds, teachers, etc. Therefore, in some places we employ the use of "I" or "my" for example. Then there are other sections that indicate a joint belief or opinion, and there we use "we" or "our." In any case, we believe that you, the reader, can relate to the information, regardless of which one of us actually wrote that section, or who the situation relates to.

Disclosures

As you read this book, keep in mind that part of what we are attempting to do is assist you with learning how to manage your money more wisely. Given the uncertainty of life, including such things as expanding or contracting financial markets, health issues, and time, no one, including us, can guarantee any profit or protect against losses. All information contained in this book is not intended to be used and must not be used as a basis for any tax, legal, medical, accounting, or investment advice. You should consult professional advisors on these matters, and always make informed decisions.

Given this, we firmly believe you should take what we have to share and apply whole-heartedly to your life. These ideas can be very beneficial to you. We have applied them and have put them into practice in our own lives. We also know how successful and wealthy (both defined by how happy you are with what you have) you too may become by applying not all, but just a few of our tips, suggestions, and strategies. We get extremely excited when we think about how much greater/wealthier the people of the world could be if they would just apply and appreciate the simple and most common of things to their own lives.

CHAPTER ONE
Introduction to the Game

Money is simple. The concepts do not change. The rules apply in all situations. Down to a very simple example, two plus two always equals four. The only things that people can do with their money are either—save it—or spend it. It doesn't get any simpler than that. In the game of basketball, all you have to do is dribble, pass and shoot. However, there are those in professional basketball that are earning multi-millions of dollars. Therefore, they must be dribbling, passing and shooting a little better than most people do in their driveway. Money can be viewed in the same way. Even though all we do with it is spend it or save it, there are those who tend to be better at managing it.

We are writing these words to help you apply basic financial concepts to improve your current financial situation and other means of gaining wealth—to be explained more fully in future chapters. This includes meeting your desires, goals, and gaining a better understanding of money, and obtaining a new level of satisfaction out of what you have now and will obtain in the future. This book is for everyone, written to help him or her to avoid financial uncertainty in the world today. Read this next sentence carefully: information that is valuable is information that is valuable to you. It relates to helping you meet your specific goals, whether financial or otherwise, not just being frugal.

Glean from the words in this text what should, and must, apply to you. Some ideas will fit your situation and others won't.

There are some that you must apply, those which may be a sacrifice or stretch, but will greatly improve your situation and outcome.

We would like to convey to you that **wealth is individually defined, and is measured by how happy or satisfied you are with what you've got.** Once more, how happy are you with what you have? You may be worth tens of thousands or even hundreds of thousands of dollars and still be unhappy. Conversely, you may have a financial net worth far less, and be extremely happy.

From our point of view, money is a game. It is a game that everyone plays. Everyone starts at a young age, with influences from parents, other family members, teachers, friends, and eventually employers and a variety of outside world sources. You must understand the objective of this game. In most games the goal is whoever has the most at the end wins. Others would say that the main thing is to have fun. Money is no different. Some would say that in order to win the money game, you would have to have the most, the biggest pile, the largest estate, etc. Others would say it does not matter how much money that you have, it's what you are able to do with it that matters most. But at the end, we define the success as being satisfied with what you have and the good (for yourself and others) that you do with it.

Some people are passively participating in the money game, but some participate directly. Think of a football game at the stadium. The audience is passively participating—buying tickets and concessions and cheering—but the football industry is participating directly—controlling the money that drives the games and the teams and sponsors. Some people passively participate in society—having a job, buying things, and paying bills—yet exercise no real control over their money or spending. Others take control, have a plan, define goals, and achieve a sense of well-being that is very solid and fulfilling.

There is competition on all levels. Many of the players or participants just want to get by, survive day to day. Others want to be comfortable and maintain a certain lifestyle. Finally, there's a group that wants to win everything at all costs. Pick your spot. This book will help you define where you are now in this picture, where you want to be in the future, and how to get there.

You get to decide how you want to play this game. It is a long process, and there are many timeouts and pauses. Sometimes you will be able to determine who the players are, and at other times they will be determined for you. There will be team members, different leagues, and adversaries. In the money game, these include your family, friends, co-workers, salesmen, bankers, insurance agents, and employers. All of these have an impact on the outcome.

There may be times when you are in control of the game and have the opportunity to change or enhance the rules. And other times that you may be penalized or have to play by rules determined by others.

The exciting thing about the money game is that you get to determine the objective. Is your objective to have fun, to accumulate the most, to give the most away? It does not matter. You are in charge, or at least can be much more in control by the choices that you make. You get to determine if you are actively involved in the game, or on the sidelines taking a break, pausing. Even by being a spectator at times, you are involved at a given level. The important thing to understand is that *you are participating*, and that everything else happening around you will influence your level of success. In this game, it is up to you to determine what success is—as everyone will define their own level of that success.

Understand your options. Relate a human aspect to the financial concepts. During sour times, make lemonade.

Ask anyone what the word "wealth" means to them and almost everyone will envision a materialistic lifestyle. That lifestyle includes such things as fancy cars, big houses, extensive travel, and all sorts of do-dads. The proverbial Jones family—can we really keep up with them?

Again, however, having true wealth means being pleased or happy with what you have. This does not mean that you shouldn't strive to meet your monetary goals, or that you should not enjoy the journey along the way. You should, and you will, by understanding the fundamentals and implementing a few simple strategies.

CHAPTER TWO
Core Values

Several years ago, one of us wrote an essay for a niece when she graduated high school called, "Lessons Learned in Life." It was also shared with two nephews when they graduated later. It was about the important things in life. The writing also included a collection of stories, sayings, and thoughts garnered over the years. As we have said, we are writing this book about becoming wealthy and enjoying life. But, being wealthy does not mean having all of the money you want. Money is a tool, to be used wisely, not the thing that will solve all problems.

Lessons Learned in Life

We believe that there are only four important things in life. None of the four can be purchased with money and we have based much of this book on this concept.

The four necessities are FAITH, FITNESS, FAMILY, and FRIENDS. Think seriously about these. Take any one of these away, and your happiness will diminish.

FAITH is an important basis for how you stand with God, with the universe, with everything you can conceive mentally. It is a basis for value, for love, for action, for direction and fulfillment in life. Keep this aspect of your life—whatever your beliefs are regarding religion—in tune with your everyday life. Fortunately, in the United States, we live in a country where we are free to pursue our religion regardless of what our faith or beliefs are.

Good **FITNESS** (Health) is important to truly enjoy life. You are truly blessed if you feel well, and are able to do the things that you want or need to do physically and mentally. Health is something to be protected. We include such things as having adequate food, clothing and shelter, and the time and means to exercise in the fitness category as all of these are required to have good health. Health is a blessing.

FAMILY is also important. Having family, be it large or small, that cares for you, will increase your happiness and therefore your sense of wealth. Knowing your background, acceptance of your family members, and sharing good times with them will bring you joy. Family values are always more important than financial net worth. Family is a foundation.

FRIENDS are needed. Even the Bible teaches that friends are priceless. Ecclesiastes Chapter 4, Verse 10 in the Bible states: If one falls down, his friend can help him up. But pity the man who falls and has no one to help him up! (New International Version). Good friends might seem in short supply. Close relationships are needed, but sometimes it is hard to develop those. Why? The top two reasons we can come up with are 1) we are either too busy or 2) are afraid of competition. Friends should be seen as companions. They can help you with doing a job. Two working together can accomplish more than two individuals working separately. And, it is more fun! Secondly, two friends can support each other. Thirdly, friends offer warmth and understanding. If we feel down, threatened, vulnerable, etc. they can lend a shoulder to lean on. And last, they increase our strength, just as a rope of several strands is stronger than individual cords. Be a friend and you will have a friend. Friends are priceless.

Relationship Investment Averaging

We have written about the concept of **"DOLLAR COST AVERAGING"** in another section of this book. To define it briefly, it means to continue to invest your money whether the markets are rising or falling.

But have you considered that building wealth through having great relationships with your family and friends also requires a continual investment? We call this **"RELATIONSHIP INVESTMENT AVERAGING."** Everyone should continually make investments in relationships to keep them vibrant, growing and healthy. We make the following three points that are important to help you maintain and develop better relationships.

1) **Communication is always the key.** It requires effort and, sometimes, sacrifice. You must not be afraid of communicating your feelings. But you must do it in a non-threatening or non-condescending manner. And, communication on a consistent basis is required, the "investment averaging" idea. Miscommunications will require that the individuals forgive themselves and each other before the relationship moves forward. Lack of or poor communication will cause stress within the relationship, so you need to have honest and frequent conversations with the other person.

2) **Do not take a relationship for granted.** When this happens it is usually because you have forgotten about the value of the relationship or do not treasure it. Relationships will either grow, or wither and die, so don't forget to nurture them through conversation, caring, compassion, listening, etc. Invest in them frequently.

CORE VALUES

3) **Do not neglect a relationship.** We are all very busy in today's world, and time can slip away easily. A relationship requires frequent investments, so take planned steps to enhance them. Schedule time on your calendar if you must. Remember, it is not all about the amount of time spent, but also the quality. A quality friendship will endure with maintenance. Remember, it is better to eat a peanut butter sandwich with someone you want to spend time with than fancy dining on lobster with someone you do not want to be around.

Aunt Rose

I was greatly blessed for having my Aunt Rose in my life. She has been gone for several years now, and I still miss her. I believe that she was one of the wealthiest people I have ever known. She did not have a lot of money or material things, and I don't believe that it was important to her. She possessed love of family and happiness to the nth degree. If you were at her house, she shared whatever food she might have, listened to you, laughed with you, and made you feel like you were very special. Matter of fact, you were special to her.

A meal at her house could be anything from a bologna sandwich to a turkey feast. It did not matter, as her guests always left content. As long as everyone had something to eat, had the opportunity to share stories, and could play a fierce card game of ten-point pitch, she was happy. And believe me, although she liked to win her card game, I guarantee she never cheated.

I never went to Aunt Rose's house and found her without company. Everyone flocked to her door. It was the place to be. That is what true wealth is about.

CHAPTER THREE
Fundamentals

In this chapter, we identify and explain **SEVEN FINANCIAL FUNDAMENTALS** we believe to be crucial to your success in the game. Each one of these will have an impact on your score, and are briefly outlined as follows:

1) **Responsibility**—Again, it is you that must take **ownership** of your game actions.

2) **Income**—You must have a source of funds, which translates as your **offense**.

3) **Live within your means**—This relates to watching all of your plays—being in **control** of your spending habits, be it either needs or wants.

4) **Emergency Fund**—Understand you must **posture** yourself at all times to avoid letting someone else (the other team, i.e. those demanding your money) to gain the upper hand.

5) **Time Value of Money**—This play will allow you to **capitalize** on the funds you have or the investments that you have already made.

6) **Dollar Cost Averaging**—The theory of dollar cost averaging will help you gain an **advantage** for a better return on your efforts.

7) **Protection**—When you gain control of your game, it is imperative that you **defend** those game points, through well planned insurance coverage.

Responsibilities = Ownership

Fundamentals
- **Income = Offense**
- **Live Within Your Means = Control**
- **Emergency Fund = Posture**
- **Time Value of Money = Capitalize**
- **Dollar Cost Averaging = Advantage**
- **Protection = Defense**

When it comes to building your net worth, it is ultimately you who must take ownership and become the master of all of your resources. By now you should know that money is a very simple thing. You will either spend it or save it. Both can bring you joy and satisfaction. However, neither one will define your (net) worth.

Acting your age when it comes to money can be simple. We all have our obligations we must meet. The thing is that they are our own responsibilities. They are not responsibilities of our friends, our families, or the government. They are our own responsibilities. Take care of them yourself. Life will be much more in control. Be responsible. Examples of responsibilities may and will vary from one to another because once again they are "your" responsibilities. Your car payment is your responsibility. Your house payment or your rent, your utilities, your phone bill, cell bill, and cable bill are your responsibility. Your emergency fund is your responsibility. Your retirement funds are definitely and ultimately your responsibility.

Ultimately YOU will be accountable for the decisions you make and this accountability will be reflected in the future ability to make even more and greater decisions. Your credit score is an obvious example of how each of us are held accountable. It is a reflection of how well you make payments, whether or not YOU tend to overextend yourself, and even how prudent you are with your finances. Even the responsibility of protecting the rating itself is on your shoulders. With identity theft rampant today you must be on guard to protect what you have worked so hard for.

You must come to the realization that you are responsible for your decisions and solely accountable for the results and the position that you put yourself in. Also, you get to ask yourself whether or not you are happy with what you are earning. Key areas to concentrate on include taxes, retirement, debt and income. In order to succeed in these areas, you are responsible to continually educate yourself in all of these areas.

This is a good news, bad news situation. The good news is you do not have to depend on anyone else to accomplish all you want to in the world when it comes to finances. The bad news is that it is indeed in your hands.

Responsibilities = Ownership
Income = Offense
Live Within Your Means = Control
Emergency Fund = Posture
Time Value of Money = Capitalize
Dollar Cost Averaging = Advantage
Protection = Defense

Source of Income

Now that you have taken on the responsibility to master each fundamental, it is important to create a great offense. This will allow you to accomplish whatever you set out to achieve. For example, unless you are independently wealthy, or a trust fund baby, you must have income (AKA a job) to support yourself—to pay for the needs and wants. It is good to work. It provides purpose in life, keeps people out of trouble, and can be very fulfilling. One of our fathers worked until the age of 90, when a stroke forced him to quit. He always said that he wanted to keep on working, because if he didn't, he wouldn't be able to.

In some cases a job is self-employment or small business ownership, and that requires much more self discipline and responsibility. Also, it involves substantial risk, like losing everything and having to start over. If you're already in a successful business, good for you. If you're not, be very careful about starting one. Unless you're very careful about it, or already doing it successfully, you could lose everything at some point in the future. Know the risks. They are usually extremely high.

To get ahead, you must not only have a job, but consistently keep a job. Yes, you can change jobs for a bigger salary or wage, or to advance your career, or to possibly change careers, and that can be a good thing, but you still must have it.

A job is a big part of the game. It is YOUR means by which to accomplish goals and objectives. It is a primary responsibility. You learn some of the rules for a job by going to school and studying for your vocation, however, most are acquired on the job. An integral part of a job is knowing how to keep it. Consider: hard work, loyalty, continuous learning, manners, showing up on time, and teamwork. And don't forget good communication.

Even if you are self-employed, all of the above still fit in. You must satisfy your customers, government regulations, and societal rules. To win, you must be consistent and play the game to a large degree of satisfaction.

Individual Income

I knew a person who had a college degree in accounting. He obtained an entry-level position after moving to a new town, and established himself with a company as a good employee who was reliable, could make contributions to the team, and was overall an asset to the company. The situation was that it was an entry-level position. This person was going to have to work his way up through the ranks. Pay his dues. He was in communication with management and would indeed get a "good" pay raise when it came that time of the year when they were "handed out."

The problem with this was that this person had already been in the industry for five years with his previous employer. He had already gained experience previously but that job had not yielded the career and payoff this individual had wanted. Now, instead of being five years into a good career, he was back to where he started from regardless of what the company thought of him. So what happened? This individual asked for a raise. He asked for this after just ninety days of employment. How could the company respond? How should the company respond? They communicated that they appreciated this employee. That he was an asset to the team and come evaluation time he would be positively rewarded for his efforts based on his continued positive performance with the company.

This was not good enough for this individual. Who said it should be? This person with five years of experience had all the rights in the world to respectfully ask for greater consideration.

This person could change jobs. He could look for other employment that would take into consideration the experience brought to the table.

This person could also evaluate the situation and consider even more options. Change jobs and careers altogether. Go back to school and learn something else that would pay more. What we are really talking about here is pay. How much can I make and am I satisfied with it? For this individual it was not enough. He was in the process of trying to earn more. He was willing to take the chance on what the additional schooling would yield.

I also knew a gentleman who worked with me for several years. Once again it was in the field of accounting. We were both hired around the same time and began our accounting careers at about the same level. We worked together for over three years when the company began to experience changes in the market and made some decidedly apparent decisions to cut back the accounting work force significantly.

We were both let go about the same time. The interesting part was what decisions we both made over the next few months. I made the decision to retrench in the field of accounting and gain experience in different areas. I felt I needed to learn and experience more of each area of accounting to be a more valuable employee.

My friend took another approach, being a couple of years younger and highly intelligent (this was apparent because he was able to get out of college in three years). Anyway, he was no dummy. However, he still found himself in a tough position—newly married and uncertain as to what to do with his career. Should he retrench and become the entry-level accountant once again? We have heard how this could come out. I have experienced it myself. For the record, retrenching is not good. It is just that, retrenching. Sure, you may shore up some weaknesses and that may be necessary, but nonetheless, you do lose some ground.

As for my friend, in trying to figure out what to do, he took a test. That's right; since he did not know what he personally wanted to do, he found an aptitude test that was able to guide him based on his skills, interests, and abilities. Based on the scoring of this test, it suggested that he pursue something in the medical field. And correspondingly with his level of intellect, etc., that he specifically become a pharmacist. So that is what he did. He went back to school for several years and became a pharmacist. He and his wife had to make some decidedly difficult decisions to retrench—decisions to not spend much, not travel much, to live in a smaller house, cook more macaroni and cheese, etc. However, the sacrifices were worth it. Today he makes a great living and he is doing fine. This is just an example of how to determine what your earnings should be, and also, how to deal with determining what and how to earn money.

It does not change, however, the fundamental, absolute fact that you must live within your means—no matter what that is.

FUNDAMENTALS Control

Fundamentals

Responsibilities = Ownership
Income = Offense
Live Within Your Means = Control
Emergency Fund = Posture
Time Value of Money = Capitalize
Dollar Cost Averaging = Advantage
Protection = Defense

Each game will volley from offense to defense. Therefore it is critical that each one stay in control and learn to effectively manage these transitions when they occur. This is accomplished by being disciplined throughout the game. We have been motivated to write this book for a reason. People are time and time again getting away from one of the most basic principles of financial rules. As this is brought up, your response might be, "Well, duh," or, "That's a no-brainer," or "That's just common sense." It sure has hit the headlines in many news articles, financial magazines, and editorials, but the truth of the matter is that most people are not following this rule. When I think of how basic this is, I think of the famous quote of Vince Lombardi when he started every football season by addressing his team by holding up a football to them and saying, "This is a football." It did not matter how many years his player had played with him; he always started the season the same way. He wanted to leave no doubt that the game of football at whatever level was a game of basics.

The same holds true when it comes to money, and the biggest basic that applies is that you cannot spend more than you make. This is a truth and where we must start. **By definition YOU CANNOT DEBT SPEND i.e. Do not use your CREDIT CARDS if you cannot pay them off at the end of the month.** Ask yourself the following question, "What are my earnings?" Bottom line, we mean the **NET** amount of your paycheck. You may have additional sources of income, but we want to keep this as simple as possible for everyone in this example. This sounds so easy, or so basic. However, as we make this attempt at clarification there are so many things that muddy the waters on both how much one might have to spend and what things people spend their money on. Even though we know this is the most basic of the fundamental rules, it may be the most difficult to accomplish. So we remind you of the **KISS THEORY**, and encourage you to **"KEEP IT SO SIMPLE."** YOU can do it. YOU as well as those around you are counting on YOU. We want to share what it takes to get it done. So let's get started.

1. **Take your paycheck stub and locate the net pay figure. That is how much you have to spend.**

2. **Do not spend more than that!**

Boy, it sounds so simple. The fact of the matter is it can be very difficult. We all seem to have more "rainy" days than what we have saved for, or at least they seem to last a lot longer than the "sunny" days we have used to get ahead in the game.

We are all bombarded with advertisements of things we "must" spend our money on. For example, there are so many good restaurants that we love to frequent or that are "new" and we must try. And the ability to spend money you don't have skyrockets as "consumers" are bombarded with "free money," the money à la credit card game. Even people with poor credit are offered cards in the weekly mail. Of course, the real cost is deadly: high interest rates, acceleration clauses for cash advances, free "checks," late fees, a deadly financial trap with the allure of status. For those tempted or already trapped, **wake up, everyone! This is someone else playing his or her money game. This is their means. The more they "sell" to you the more they have to spend. Do you want to win the game or be the loser?**

Currently, research shows that over 42 percent of Americans spend more than they make. I was astounded by this and thought surely the overspending could not have been by much. However, in fact it turns out that the same 42 percent of people are outspending their income by over 20 percent.

This book is not about getting rich by making a bunch of money. It is about creating wealth and living a great life. Anyone can do it! Everyone gets to define it. It's about being happy with what you've got. That is what the measure of wealth is. "How happy you are is directly reflected in your attitude." Your attitude is a function of how happy you are. Do you need to change your attitude? It takes discipline to change your attitude. Maybe you are totally unhappy with what you've got. Great, perhaps that is just the motivation you need to begin developing the discipline

FUNDAMENTALS
Control

necessary to change your attitude regarding what it takes for you to be happy.

Maybe you should be happy with what you've got. Perhaps all you need is a change of perspective. Maybe to the majority of people you have "everything." What is everything? Keep in mind **"Faith, Fitness, Family, and Friends."** If you've got these, you've got it all. Take any one out of the equation and where is your happiness?

It is so easy to take one or more of these for granted. First, let's consider **Fitness**. As long as we are feeling well … who cares? This is especially true when we are young. However, as you get older, even though your eyesight seems to fade, the appreciation for your health and physical fitness definitely becomes clearer and clearer.

It is also amazing, when challenged with a health issue, how quickly life snaps back into perspective and we immediately reprioritize. My daughter recently hit her chin while riding her bike. It only took a split second for the most important thing for our family to do that day was to get her to the hospital. It did not matter who needed a bath, or if it was bedtime. The most important thing was her health and welfare. We took care of it. "Money" did not matter, the world just stopped and health was the immediate priority.

Then there is **Family**. How common is it to take them for granted? We shouldn't. Many families have been broken apart because they have taken one another for granted. Respect. That is what we all want. I know my mother did while she was alive. She asked for it from my father, she asked for it from my sisters and myself, and I know she asked for it from her second husband. My wife asked me for it today. She asked for it from our children. I do love and respect her. She has been my guiding light from the moment we met. I have always told people that she did my homework in college. This is not true. We both were studying accounting and it was immediately obvious to me that she was better than I was. She was great at getting her own homework done. She did not do mine; I simply copied hers. I respect her abilities and always have. Honestly, though, together we have brought two lovely children into the world, have provided them with opportunities, given them all the love we can muster, and they are truly the joys of our lives. Do not take family for granted—it is your life.

FRIENDS are the same way. Friends are also harder to come by than family. Families are created and there is a bond there that will never break no matter what in the world happens. Friends on the other hand can be lost, and lost forever. This can be painful. I have lost friends for no good reason. Time itself causes friends to drift apart. They may still be in your heart, but not in your life. So much can be lost. These relationships, as with family relationships, must be maintained and appreciated. Appreciation, empathy, and respect, are all things that a good relationship must have to grow and prosper.

A good friend of mine pointed out that deposits must be made into a friendship in order to occasionally make withdrawals. I would agree with that—that a friendship is a two-way street. There is give and take. No one should be taken advantage of or it will fade away.

Then there is **FAITH**. Definitely taken for granted at times. Even in the completion of this book, we found ourselves placing the "Faith" concept in this section at the end instead of following our earlier layout of priorities, which demonstrated to us sometimes

FUNDAMENTALS
Control

taking one's faith for granted. God is always there and we are truly thankful. We know we are. But just maybe that is what is taken for granted. We know in our hearts that He is always there. So what do we do? Just look at the church attendance rosters for Christmas and Easter compared to the rest of the year. What is happening? We're just going about our business. We are so busy; we have so many other priorities. Yes, we take it for granted. We live in the greatest country in the world that allows us to worship our Lord in our own way. Do it! Do not take it for granted. Appreciate it and thank the Lord.

Fundamentals

Responsibilities = Ownership
Income = Offense
Live Within Your Means = Control
Emergency Fund = Posture
Time Value of Money = Capitalize
Dollar Cost Averaging = Advantage
Protection = Defense

You must posture yourself to have a readiness for any situation. The ability to execute the quickness necessary in maintaining your status is critical. Quickness in the financial sense is maintaining liquidity in the form of emergency funds. Everyone talks about this but does YOUR emergency fund really exist? When you are starting out, it is not the amount in your emergency fund but the high importance of developing **HABITS** to develop and maintain it. Start small, do what you can, and put it in a safe place. Start with the change in your pockets. Empty your pockets every day into a hidden place such as behind the spices in the kitchen. Saving one's change is one of the best habits to develop. This works. Keep doing it. Forever. Take it seriously. These funds can and should be directed to a purpose.

Strive for a solid emergency fund—until six to nine months of living expenses have been accumulated.

Debt and budgeting enter into the equation when considering and establishing an emergency fund. As for the matter of debt, it won't skyrocket if you have funds to turn to in the event of an emergency.

This brings us to: What is an emergency, anyway? As a responsible adult, an honest person, and one with established goals and a plan, you must truly define "emergency." For the most part, there should be no surprises. **So what we're talking about could be better classified as non-routine expenditures.** For many years I have referred to an emergency fund as my "water heater account." I think this is more accurate than another example I have used as the "new set of tires" account. The "water heater" label is more accurate because even though you might anticipate someday needing a new water heater, you truly do not know when. A "new set of tires" on the other hand can be more easily anticipated. You can check your tires and know within a few months that you will need a new set. At that point you can begin to plan for the expenditure.

LET'S LIST A FEW ITEMS THAT CAN BE CONSIDERED EMERGENCIES:

    1) **Water heater**

    2) **Medical services, i.e. stitches for a cut chin**

    3) **Loss of job**

    4) **Short-term disability**

AND A FEW THAT ARE NOT TRULY EMERGENCIES:

    1) **New set of tires**

    2) **Birthday gifts**

    3) **Christmas shopping**

    4) **Impulse buying**

FUNDAMENTALS
Posture

As your fund grows, your financial stress level goes down. If you currently spend $3,000 per month on living expenses, your emergency fund should be at the very minimum $9,000 (e.g. 3 months times $3,000). For example, you could keep a $1,000 or so at home in a safe place, which is very liquid (meaning very accessible—no fees to access, etc.) Next, save an amount that could be in the form of a $2,000 savings account plus a couple of short term 30 day CDs of $3,000 each. What we are saying is, the first month, you have readily accessible funds with no withdrawal fees associated. The next two months, the CDs will come due and will become accessible without fees and without penalties within 30 days. These normally can be set up at your bank to renew for another 30 days automatically, so you do not have to constantly monitor them.

Then, at this point, your goal should be to get to a six-month level of emergency funds (adding a couple more CDs, which can be 60 day terms or in money market accounts of some sort).

Bottom line, this is great in theory, and having the goal of a six to nine month emergency fund is necessary, but the fact is, when an emergency hits, all bets are off and it becomes a true function of liquidity. The question becomes, where are the funds? Currently, too many people are having to tap into their retirement accounts or college savings accounts in order to meet their daily necessities, because other funds are not available (or at least not readily accessible).

Along with this tapping into retirement funds will come possible taxes, fees, and penalties that you will want and need to avoid.

It is recommended, however, when you arrive at the three-month level of savings, you should shore up other items as well. What kind of short term and long term disability insurance do you have? Do you have a couple of weeks of food and essential supplies stored in your house? These items can be helpful in a time of crisis. Maybe you are sick and just cannot or do not feel like shopping as much for a short period.

Relating the above example to your personal situation, include the following in your emergency needs: HOUSING, FOOD, UTILITIES, INSURANCE, TRANSPORTATION and MEDICAL NEEDS. Understand, when calculating what these needs are that your discretionary spending (wants) must decrease accordingly during any trying times.

Once again, be reminded of how important it is to have a certain amount of money set aside that is not earmarked for anything. That is what an emergency fund is. Money for nothing. Nothing in particular that is.

We have talked about funds set aside for a medical emergency as an example. Going back to the earlier example of a cut to the chin that required a trip to the emergency room, I am fortunate enough to work for a company that provides health insurance. However, with the skyrocketing costs of health care I still found that the emergency deductible was $200. Not the kind of money that the average person has in their pocket as change. That is where the emergency fund comes in. Yes, we could handle it without missing a car payment, without taking a hit to our credit rating, etc.

This story is not over. It had been a month or two since the incident, and I found out that the doctor had a separate bill that went along with the $200. All in all, a trip to the emergency room ended up costing almost $500. I can tell you, this was not in my budget for the month. It drives home the ultimate necessity to have funds set aside.

The thing is you never know when something like that is going to happen. Furthermore, you do not know what the actual cost is going to be. Sure, you can anticipate a lot, and you can calculate a worst-case scenario, but you just do not know.

The next thing to consider is that just because something financially trying presents itself in the form of an emergency does not mean that you are through an emergency period. The fact is, something else could happen right behind it. This is why the more we consider how much is enough, we keep coming back to the amount of six to nine months of living expenses. There may be times where this is indeed excessive. However, it does not hurt to err on the conservative side. Better safe than sorry. Better to exercise true responsibility for your own actions and situations which you might either put yourself in or find yourself in.

The amount of your emergency fund can also be in relation to the type of lifestyle you live. If you and your family are one of high energy and recreation, one that exposes itself to greater risks, etc., you may want to increase the fund amount. If you have a career that is more volatile—such as sales or commission-based earnings—or one that is cyclical in nature, this too may require a more conservative approach and higher amounts. However, if your career is ultimately stable and secure—with a very predictable income—you may not need to have so much saved up.

Regardless of the amount, you must put it in a place that is considered to be untouchable. This may be more difficult for some than others. Some may be able to have three or four hundred dollars in their wallet and never touch it. For others, if you have more than twenty dollars you are definitely going to spend it. Depending on your personality, you may need to put these funds in a more remote location.

We have discussed this in detail and we have come to the conclusion that the average person will not have the discipline to have three to six months of living expenses in their checking account and be able to keep their hands off of it. It will inevitably be spent, maybe on a house repair, or a weekend excursion. Maybe on a gift for a deserving loved one, but nevertheless it will disappear under normal circumstances.

That is why it is recommended to have a separate savings account set up for this purpose. A money market account that has earnings potential would work well for this. I try to set accounts up that automatically draw from a checking account that can be easily fit into the normal budget. You want this fund to always grow just as your earnings and net worth grow. Depending on earnings, and how much these funds are drawn upon, you can expect it to fluctuate between three and six months of living expenses. If you are fortunate enough and or cautious enough to avoid emergencies, you may find yourself able to have saved enough to help fund other desires.

Fundamentals

Responsibilities = Ownership
Income = Offense
Live Within Your Means = Control
Emergency Fund = Posture
Time Value of Money = Capitalize
Dollar Cost Averaging = Advantage
Protection = Defense

When it comes to money and finances nothing is more critical than time. Just as we must protect our credit rating from identity theft, we must protect one of our greatest resources—time— from being wasted away. The key to this is getting your money (assets) working for you as early as possible. Early in the game we work hard for money … later in the game the goal is to have it

FUNDAMENTALS
Capitalize

working hard for us. No matter where you currently happen to be financially, you have got to do the first thing first. Today is always the first day of the rest of your life. When you can understand the "time" value of money, it will become clear to you exactly what must be done first. Time after time, again and again, we have been told or we have read that we must "pay ourselves first." Get your money working (invested) for you.

Most people in our country settle for much less than they could potentially earn. Why? Several reasons. Many just simply are uneducated. We as a nation have failed to teach basic fundamentals of finances. Remember back to high school. We will wager that you learned how to dissect a frog or some other animal. How many times have you used that knowledge since? Thought so. On the flip side, were you taught about savings, investments, insurance, retirement, estate planning, or other pertinent financial subjects? Didn't think so.

Other reasons we settle for less are just plain laziness or lack of discipline. Also, people tend to follow the instant gratification school of thought. Why save for later if you can enjoy now? Never mind peace of mind, being debt free, having more to spend later, etc.

It is time that you learn. **Time to start saving. Time to start investing. You have to start and the time is NOW.** Forget about the wealth of others, it does not change your current financial status. Yes, the wealthy get wealthier. They ARE getting wealthier. Money allows you to build it even more. Simple mathematics—get it?

Many millionaires are first generation millionaires, meaning that they earned their own money and saved and invested. It wasn't given to them. They started small and built funds gradually over a period of time. And, they have taken more than one avenue, using different types of investing. But bottom line, they have not made the mistake of doing nothing. They started the process. They took the first step toward a specific, written goal. And they kept at it by investing for growth, took advantage of what our government offered, and set their sights on the long-term rewards.

The rewards will be there if you resign yourself to discipline. It is a requirement! Sacrifice, patience and perseverance all come to mind. A million dollars might be your goal. This might seem a large number at first, but when you see the logic of how to achieve this number over time, you can see how you can have a very good chance of obtaining this number! Maybe just getting out of debt is your goal. It is your game, you decide. Again, this book is about being wealthy, not just financially, but about being happy with what you have, about what you are doing, about what you give away, about your relationships, etc. Back to the large number mentioned above, yes, there are lots of variables in your game. Obviously the basic economy, your age, your earnings potential, and the actions of the stock market are big factors. However, over a long period of time, e.g. the 40 years of your career addressed in the following paragraphs, that goal is certainly a possibility, especially when considering the "average rate of return" of the market over that period of time. Again, there are no guarantees, in life or in financial returns. Just do your research, keep investing, take advantage of tax savings, and don't give up!

We do not seek to tell you how to win big in the stock or bond market, what to invest in, or how to win at the bank or the casino. We are telling you to start the process, develop savings habits, invest somewhere reasonable, keep your focus on long-term goals, and prepare to enjoy your efforts.

Fundamentals
Capitalize

Many things are out of your control, such as the current state of the economy (good or bad), health issues, job situations, etc. But, everyone faces these challenges. **All "ordinary" people have the potential to win big with consistent saving and investing discipline.** Get started—you will be glad you did. It is a sure thing—once you start and stick to the plan—that you will have a much greater chance of success.

I have always felt that one's earning years, span or length of career is 40 years. I do not know when I picked it up or why that is but that is the length of time I have based my calculations on. Maybe it is just because the math is easy. It is a nice round period of time that you can use to base your figures. A time period that is long enough to allow money to work for you but yet short enough to at least get a feeling that you do not have to work forever if you "play your cards right."

It would seem reasonable that most people can get out of high school and get a "job" by age 20. You can then expect that with reasonably good health you will be able to work until age 60 and in today's terms be able to call it "early retirement." Based on that, it would mean that you should expect to be actively earning and making a living for 40 years. If one chooses to go to college and gets to work at age 24 or 26 years old it also can be reasonable to expect with those greater earnings capabilities to be able to "make up" the delayed 4 to 6 years of earnings, or, at the worst, push retirement to age 64 or 66.

Forty years it is. That is the length of time the average person can expect to work in today's economic conditions. We have even heard that overnight success takes 40 years, so that is what we are talking about—overnight success. How exciting is that? Great, we knew we could do it! We can tell everyone how to achieve overnight success, or how to "get rich quick." Not really, but we can help you develop methods to give you a much better chance of achieving that success.

We have used 40 years because that will be a long enough working time for most of us to achieve our investment goals. Once you define this as the amount of time you have to earn, you will have an understanding of how much you must accomplish and by when. That may be all that some people need to know. What is the length of the game? When is it over? When does it end? Or, when can it end?

Now that you know how long you will be playing, you can start the game. Oh, and the game has begun, believe me. Have you put yourself in?

If you think like me and you get the sense that there is no way you will work that long, you may want to try to figure out how to shorten the time frame. I will leave setting those goals up to you. The clue would be to make the most of your time … carpe diem, or whatever you need to do to get a move on. Do not be discouraged if you are not in your 20s or 30s (40s or 50s). It is never too late to begin a plan to reach your selected goals.

A lot of things fit this time frame. Kids can be raised. A 30-year mortgage can be paid off, etc.

LET'S GET STARTED AND SET SOME "GOALS AND OBJECTIVES." LET'S UNDERSTAND OUR RULES:

1) **Time is of the essence.**
2) **If you are going to pay off a home in 30 years it must be purchased by age 30, or you must accelerate the mortgage, or use some retirement dollars to do so, etc.**
3) **Retirement must be saved for by age 60.**

FUNDAMENTALS
Capitalize

We'll start with just these three and you can add and delete as necessary. It's your game. Have some fun. Set some goals, dream a little, enjoy. It seems like all of this is just common sense, but to me, it seems even more common that people don't even know that they are playing the game, and that in fact they are critically behind on the scoreboard and losing—maybe even being taken advantage of by other players in the game that don't mind stepping all over them.

It's like growing a tree. I have moved into a couple of neighborhoods over the years and know that people like trees. However, even though people want trees in their yards, they do not get them planted very quickly. I have seen people live in a neighborhood three, five and even seven years before they plant one. In talking to them they know it takes years for a tree to grow to any size. The exciting thing about a tree is that once you plant it, the hard work is done. All that is left to do is to begin having the enjoyment of watching it grow, and pruning it occasionally to keep it on the straight and narrow path upwards. There is also the peace of mind that you have done all you can do to get it to grow. Sure, you can water it and nurture it some but for the most part it is out of your hands. You have done what you need to do to get it to grow. Admit it, the growth of a tree is up to what nature has to offer. But, if it does not get planted it can never get started with its natural growth.

Retirement funding is the same as that tree. Retirement savings take years to grow. However, just like planting that tree, getting started is the hardest thing to do, and it is your responsibility to do it. It is exciting as well because once you get started, all you have to do is watch it grow. I am referring to setting up an IRA or signing up for your company's 401(k) plan—any systematic retirement savings account. You also must accept the fact that the growth is primarily dependent on general economic market conditions, the nature of the market movements which are out of your control. It is like weather conditions that affect the planted tree. There are some things you can do to "nurture" it as well to make it as healthy as possible and we will be covering this as well.

The issue here is time: getting started and making the most of it. How much time do we have? We do not know. What we do know is that it is limited. There are only so many hours in the day, days in the year, years to take advantage of, etc. We have to know whether or not we are making the most of our time. When it comes to finances the foundation is the **"TIME VALUE OF MONEY."** What is the value of money? Things are worth more today than tomorrow … maybe if you are talking about a depreciable asset. I have found that to grasp the idea behind the "time value of money" concept it is best to fully understand a certain RULE. This certain rule is very simple, as most rules or laws are. I know a lot of people have heard of it and do understand it. But I am trying to share it with those who don't. **I am so adamant about it that if you can only pick this book up for a second and grasp only this concept and get it applied in your personal life, the book has set you on a course of great success.** As I have said, it is simple. It is called **THE RULE OF 72**. That's all that some of you need to recall as you know the rule and are putting it to use. There is a second group that is made up of those of you who have heard of the rule and maybe even understand it but you have not applied it to your own lives. Therefore, you do not fully understand the RULE. Then there is a third group that is saying to themselves, "The Rule of What?" Let me explain. Mathematically, a rule is just that. A rule. To further

FUNDAMENTALS
Capitalize

clarify this, it is a matter of fact. It has been proven and works every time. Just like gravity, it doesn't need much explanation—it just works all the time—all day, every day.

So how does it work? Simple. **It is the rule that tells you how soon it will take your money to double no matter what rate of return you are getting on your investment.** Just divide that rate of return into "72." If you are getting 1% divide that into "72," to find that it will take 72 years for that investment to double. Now this may or may not sound exciting but it can be useful and very powerful. Take 3% for example. A $10,000.00 investment will be worth $20,000.00 in 24 years and $40,000.00 in 48 years. Now pay attention. The same $10.000.00 at 12% vs. 3% will be worth $160,000.00 in 24 years, not $20,000.00, and it will be worth $256,000.00 at 12% vs. 3% in 48 years, not $40,000.00. This might be a good spot for some of you to get a pen and paper and perform a few calculations on your own to see just how exciting this "RULE" can be. For others you might take a few minutes and figure how much debt you might have from the $3,000.00 balance you have on that credit card at 18%. It just might be worth taking the passbook savings you have earning 1.25% or less and paying it off this month.

Talk about putting out a fire, this is a fire to put out now. Now you know why credit card companies make a fortune, and why that 18% or 21% interest makes them so much more money on "their" investment. Divide 21 into 72 and you will see that every 3.43 years, their money doubles. So they can afford to drive a few into bankruptcy and lose on those people, because their money doubles so fast and at the expense of those who feed the credit machine.

The Rule of 72

Applied to a One Time Lump Sum Investment of $5,000

Interest Rate		3%	6%	12%
Years to Double (72÷Rate)		24	12	6
Year	6			$10,000
	12		$10,000	$20,000
	18			$40,000
	24	$10,000	$20,000	$80,000
	30			$160,000
	36		$40,000	$320,000
	42			$640,000
	48	$20,000	$80,000	$1,200,000

Applied to a Credit Card Balance of $1,000
(Paying interest only)

Interest Rate		6%	12%	24%
Years to Double (72÷Rate)		12	6	3
Year	3			$2,000
	6		$2,000	$4,000
	9			$8,000
	12	$2,000	$4,000	$16,000
	15			$32,000
	18		$8,000	$64,000
	21			$128,000
	24	$4,000	$16,000	$256,000

FUNDAMENTALS
Capitalize

Now, let's consider **RATE OF RETURN**. This goes along with compound interest (or compound earnings) but the point we would like to stress and somehow convey the importance to grasp is the fact that **rates of return over time are NOT LINEAR**. Once again, those of you who believe this is elementary can skip a page. That's OK, because it is elementary. Again, I am reminded, however, of the great quote of Vince Lombardi when he first addressed his players at the beginning of each season when he said while holding it up, "This is a football." Money is a game.

You must understand, grasp, and fully implement the fundamentals, and the concept here is to apply the Rule of 72. We must follow the rules as responsible adults. Understanding the Rule of 72 will catapult your rates of return. It will catapult your earnings known as compound interest (or compound earnings) to such an extent that it will no longer be referred to as compound interest. It will be referred to as "magic." Now you're saying ... what? Yes, I did say "magic." Now, I know you've heard it before ... "the magic of compound interest." Albert Einstein, the famous physicist who discovered how to unleash nuclear energy and created the famous formula $E = MC^2$, described it as MORE powerful than nuclear energy in a famous quote: **"The most powerful force in the universe is compound interest."** Think about that. Wouldn't you like to get a hold of that in your portfolio?

Your earnings obviously will grow much faster the higher the rate of return. This example does not consider any effect of income tax and assumes compounding yearly.

The significance of the rate of return should be obvious, but as I said, rates of return do not return linear results.

The Rule of 72

Applied to a One Time Lump Sum Investment of $5,000

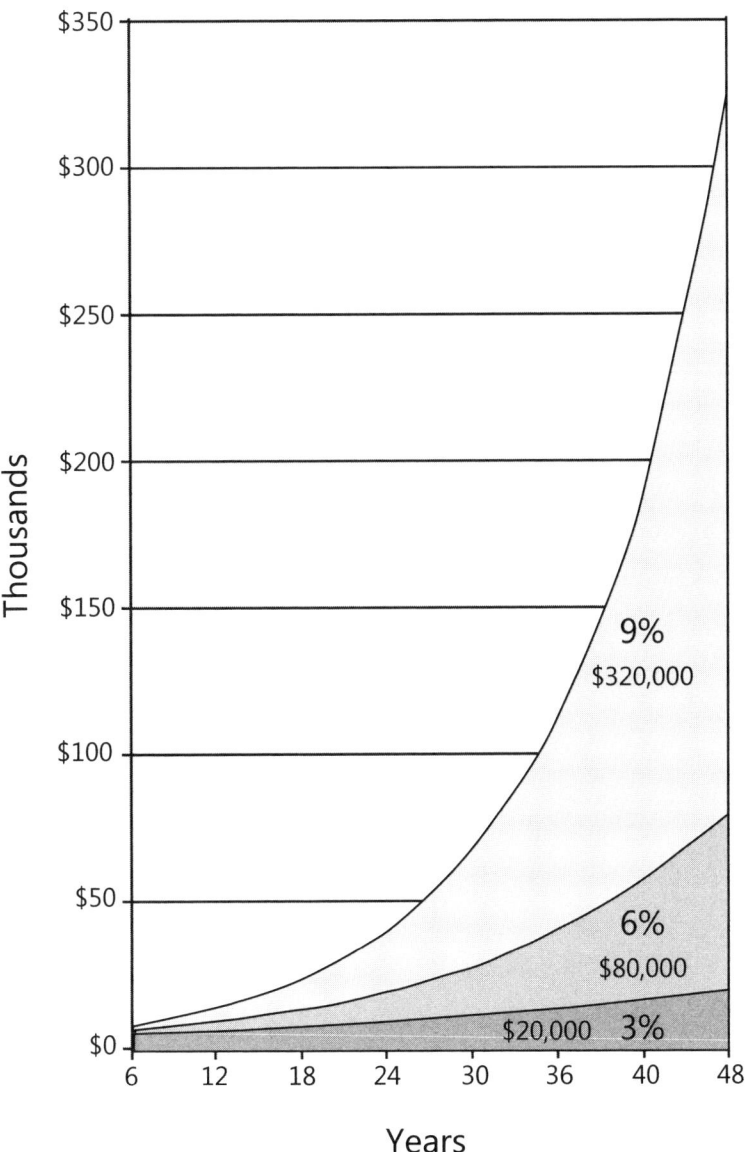

Fundamentals

Responsibilities = Ownership
Income = Offense
Live Within Your Means = Control
Emergency Fund = Posture
Time Value of Money = Capitalize
Dollar Cost Averaging = Advantage
Protection = Defense

You reach a stage in the game that you really want to get ahead. You have conditioned yourself to save. You have freed up some money in your monthly budget and from paycheck to paycheck. You have established an emergency fund and it is beginning to grow. At some point this will become a significant amount. So what's next? How do you really begin to get ahead?

Well, this is the point in the game where we distinguish a difference between saving and investing. Saving is getting that money set aside—learning how to get more value for the dollar on each and every purchase you make and every action you take. Investing is different.

THE DIFFERENCE BETWEEN SAVING AND INVESTING IS:

Saving = Setting money aside for something else.

Investing = Taking the money you have saved

and getting it to work for you.

You can have savings set aside at home earning nothing but the piece of mind that you have it, and that is truly valuable. You may also have a savings account at the local bank for a good portion of your emergency fund. This may even include some certificates of deposits. We (with our own definition) will classify them as "savings."

Now what then is investing? A good way to look at it is for "savings" you are working for dollars and then setting them aside. But investing, on the other hand, is where the money you have set aside begins to work for you. We mean work for you in a significant way. Refer back to the previous section that discusses the Rule of 72 as a very powerful force.

Dollar cost averaging is the "how (when?) to invest." Everyone has probably heard the phrase "buy low and sell high," and that makes sense. What dollar cost averaging allows one to do is to take better advantage of that concept each and every time an investment is made. Dollar cost averaging is a method of setting aside an amount (defined by you) into the same investment (chosen by you) on a consistent basis, without any regard to the current market condition. Since your contribution purchases more shares when the prices are low, and conversely less when high, your ultimate average cost per share is somewhat lower than the average cost per share.

The key to making this work is to begin to make systematic investments as soon as possible. Implementing a systematic investment strategy at age 30 will allow one to do this for 30 to 40 years if you plan to retire at an age considered "normal."

Here is how it works. Given the two investment patterns on the following page, which one would you choose? In both cases you would invest $100 each period.

Now usually it is difficult for anyone to ever willingly choose the investment pattern that will immediately let your investment total go down. It seems obvious that making an investment that increases in value period after period is the choice anyone would make.

The fact is, however, counter-intuitive. The goal over time is to consistently make investments. What that really means is that on occasion we would like to make some good buys. What makes a good buy? A cheaper price. That is what dollar cost averaging allows us to do. When the cost of the shares are down more shares are purchased and as the price decreases further, you purchase

FUNDAMENTALS
Advantage

Dollar Cost Averaging

Periodic Investment of $100

Price Per Share Each Period

Increasing Market	10	12	14	16	18	20
FluctuatingMarket	10	7	4	2	6	10

Number of Shares Purchased Each Period

							Total Shares	Total Value
Increasing Market	10.0	8.3	7.1	6.3	5.6	5.0	42.3	$845.63
Fluctuating Market	10.0	14.3	25.0	50.0	16.7	10.0	126.0	$1,259.52

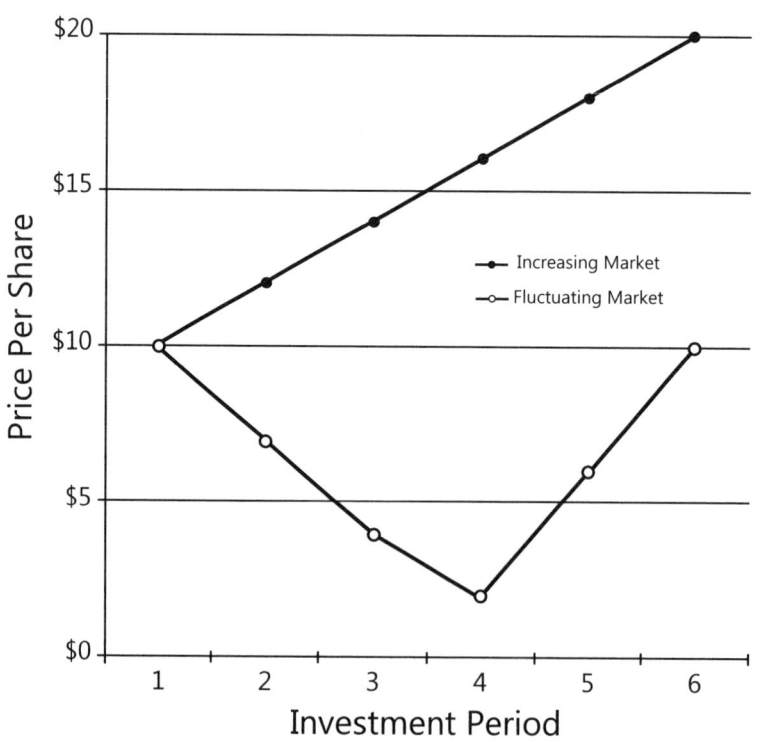

even more shares. As the price increases less shares are purchased (again, with the same consistent dollar amount invested). **What makes this work is setting up to invest consistently the same amount. This process allows an average value of the shares to be greater than the average cost of the shares.**

There are several characteristics of the market that make this advantageous. First and foremost, the average investor does not have all the money they will invest eventually all at one time. The typical investor systematically comes by extra money each and every payday. The average person does not come by windfalls, for example, very often so therefore a consistent investment makes more sense. Another reason to make systematic investments is because no one really knows when the absolute best time to invest will be. If one knew the time of the year that prices would be the lowest to invest, that would be when to make the biggest investment, but face it, we do not know that.

The one thing that we do know, however, is that the market is going to go up and down over time. That is what we want to take advantage of, and you do it by consistently investing.

Fundamentals

Responsibilities = Ownership
Income = Offense
Live Within Your Means = Control
Emergency Fund = Posture
Time Value of Money = Capitalize
Dollar Cost Averaging = Advantage

Protection = Defense

As your net worth begins to grow, there is an increasing need to protect the progress that you have made at each level. No one wants to start over, and there is no need to. It is at this point, the responsibility to defend your position is increasingly important. It is imperative to educate yourself in each of the following areas. There are several avenues to take to gain this important knowledge, and we suggest taking advantage of all of them. Included are: Classes, seminars, consultants, the Internet, etc.

Life Insurance

We believe the first rule of life insurance is not to buy it until someone becomes dependent on the insured person's earning power. For example, if you are single and just out of college, it does not make sense to purchase life insurance just to leave an estate to someone. Nor does it make sense to buy life insurance on a child, as they do not have any dependents. A general rule is to purchase enough life insurance to cover five years of normal earnings. Of course, this is up to you and also how much in premiums you can afford to pay. Don't forget to consider how much you already have in savings, or other benefits that might be available, such as Social Security survivor's benefits. Please check with your local Social Security office for help with this determination.

There are two basic types of life insurance, whole life and term insurance. As we are not going into detail in this book regarding all of the technicalities of insurance, investments, etc. we will leave it up to you to check with your insurance agent to gain knowledge on what type suits your needs. Remember that a head of a family needs the most insurance in younger years when he or she has dependents. Life insurance is a method to protect your savings and provide for your family if you die. We suggest that it could be beneficial to transition some of your savings into this protection as needed.

Health Insurance

Even though the cost of health insurance premiums continue to rise, it is important to protect your finances through purchasing this coverage. You should have insurance to cover hospitalization, other medical expenses, including doctors and surgery fees, and major medical fees. Usually, the best rates can be utilized by taking advantage of coverage offered by your employer, as insurance companies provide group rates. If you are not covered by an employer type policy, check with several insurance agents to tailor a plan that suits your needs and is the most economical.

Disability Insurance

This type of coverage is most often overlooked, but it can become very important to you if you are not able to work to provide financial needs for you and/or family. You should consider purchasing this coverage to protect yourself from loss of wages, generally up to retirement age. There are a couple of things to be certain of when purchasing a policy. Be sure that it is not cancelable and also that the definition of disability states that you are unable to work in the occupation that you have been trained. Generally, it is OK to have coverage begin a specified time after disability occurs, such as 60 or 90 days, and this will help keep the costs of premiums down. You can use your emergency funds for this first short period of time.

Homeowner's/Renter's Insurance

This insurance is for covering damages to your home and personal property and also for liability coverage for others sustaining injuries on your property. It also covers accidental damage to other people's property caused by you, or accidents originating on your property.

Remember that in general, basic homeowner's policies do not include flood or earthquake damage. Therefore, if you live in an area prone to these types of natural disasters, consider adding a rider (if available) to the policy, or a separate policy to cover any potential losses. Buy a policy that covers for replacement costs, in effect "inflation guarding." This will help protect you from inflation risks. Consider a high deductible if you can financially tolerate a bigger

FUNDAMENTALS Defense

portion of the loss, therefore reducing your annual premiums. One thing to watch out for however is the insurance company will tend to raise the coverage limits to the maximum each year when you renew the policy. Just be sure that the replacement cost coverage remains reasonable.

Automobile Insurance

This insurance covers losses for accidents (collision), natural disasters (comprehensive) and theft. Also, automobile policies cover for liability, uninsured drivers (of the other vehicle) and medical. As with all insurance, check with your insurance agent as laws vary from state to state.

Umbrella Insurance

This insurance helps cover losses arising from any damage awards not covered by your homeowner or automobile insurance or above the liability limits in those policies. In today's litigious society, it is necessary to protect yourself against these losses. Courts are awarding larger amounts of money than ever before. Ask yourself the following question: If an unfortunate accident occurs that is found to be your fault, do you have enough other insurance coverage to cover costs for negligence? Everyone should seriously consider this type of policy, as no one knows when an award may be made to someone suing you for his or her injuries. Umbrella insurance is not just for the wealthy folks of the world anymore.

Umbrella insurance will be activated when the liability limits on other current policies have been exhausted. Generally it is sold in one million dollar increments, and is reasonably cheap considering the assets (or future assets) that you are protecting. And, you are covered no matter where you might be in the world. This added layer of protection is important to your financial security.

CHAPTER FOUR
Dreams & Goals

When thinking about where you want to go in life by playing the game, don't forget to dream as part of your goal-setting process.

Dreams

Set a goal of dreaming about something that would be great to accomplish, something that you can enjoy and be proud of. When you face an unwelcome challenge, whatever that might be, keep dreaming about the things that you are setting out to do. Make this a chance to turn the situation around, in essence, make lemonade out of lemons. Whenever you get some sort of wake-up call, use it to your advantage.

Make a plan for what you want to change. Then determine what you need to do to start putting this plan into action. Follow up by taking the first steps. Any race begins with one first step, and then another, and so on. Don't forget to make adjustments as time goes on.

Flee from being the proverbial whiner. Living a life with a "down" mood will only sap your energy and provide a path for you to fail. And don't listen to others that tend to drag you down. Yes, misery sometimes likes company, but you are the one in charge—avoid those situations.

You must sometimes shift your game plan to take a new direction that will provide you with things in life that will make you better off financially, emotionally, and spiritually. Most of the time, change is difficult. Face your fears head-on. We know that can be hard to do, but if you continue to do that, each time it seems to get easier.

If you want to live a fuller life, then YOU are the one that has to change the current things that are not letting you accomplish that. Whatever it might be, YOU are the one to take steps to change. YOU cannot change everything overnight. YOU will continue to face challenges. But, it is YOU that CAN change something.

Goals

A goal is defined as a desire to reach a certain, defined accomplishment—either short-term or long-term. As part of the game to become wealthy, YOU are the one who must establish a goal or goals. And, it doesn't matter what those goals are, as long as they matter to you. Everyone will define their goals differently. Do not allow yourself to let someone else define those for you. You should define several desired accomplishments including lifestyle, health and financial. Remember, being wealthy includes all of these.

Goals can be easy to define and a process started but difficult to maintain or sustain. Just think of the diet and exercise resolutions made on January 1st each year. You must decide for yourself to set goals and make it a priority to take steps every day to keep the dream alive. Make some of the goals easy to achieve but also have several that will stretch you over a longer period. By having a set of several different types of goals, you will keep more of them alive. Small, sustained accomplishments will definitely help the long-term goals to become reality.

Editor's Note on Goals

I'm a runner. And my goal in running is and has been for decades, to run the mile in less than six minutes. Usually, I'm running it in 5:55 or 5:59. It's literally that close. When I get injured (usually not from running but from something else, like when I broke my leg in 1995), I know that even if I gain weight, even if I have to stop running for six months or a year, I know that when I start running again, and training, that eventually I will be back under six minutes. It's just a matter of time. Because—I'm running! Every day or every other day. And each day that I run, I'm closer to the 5:59 mile.

When I broke my leg, I was five months in casts. It was another three months before I could walk evenly. And I went to the track anyway, walking around it, limping in pain, eventually running 10 feet before the pain stopped me, eventually 10 yards, 100 yards, a lap, a mile in 9 minutes (how humiliating!). Guess what? In two years exactly, I ran the mile in 6:06. OK, I didn't make my goal of 5:59, but it was close enough! In another six months I was there.

And someone, a few years later, on a day when I had just finished the mile in 5:55, asked me very sarcastically, "Tell me? What do you get when you run the mile under six minutes?"

I replied with one word: "Happy."

My goals are not for everyone. My goals are for me. I set them. I live them.

If you are determined to win, you will achieve your goals. Rain. Snow. Mud. Naysayers. Heat. Joy! Joy! Joy! It's there, and not just at the end. It's there every day—joy—because you know what you did that day, and where you will be when you stay on the track.

—Jay Fraser, Editor

TO HELP YOU DEVELOP GOALS, KEEP THE FOLLOWING POINTS IN MIND:

1) **Your goal must be very specific.** Just to say "I want to retire early" or "I want to have a nice home" is not specific. You must define your goals. For example, maybe you want to have your portfolio be worth $500,000 by age 40. Or, you want to be able to have investments generate $50,000 annually beginning when you reach age 65. Or, you want to travel to six specific countries in the next six years. Bottom line, make your goals specific.

2) **Determine that your goals are truly something that you want.** It must be something that will be of importance to you or you will not spend the required time, effort, or make sacrifices to achieve it. You must decide that losing the game or failing is NOT an option. It must be specific to you, something you are passionate about. Remember to relate your goals to things you value in life—specifically, **FAITH, FITNESS, FAMILY** and **FRIENDS**—to your abilities, including financial, to sustain these relationships and desires. If you make it personal, achievable and desirable, your chances of winning the game are exponentially improved.

3) **Write them down.** Any goal that you are setting that is needing effort, sacrifice and will take some time, must be written down. No need to write down, "My goal is to not get lost driving home from work tonight." Chances are very good you will succeed in getting home. Remember that a dream is in your head and a goal is written down. Some dreams may come true, but chances are great that they *will not unless you make a plan to make them happen.*

Write goals down, and they will become like a contract, something which compels you to follow through. Write down a couple of short-term goals initially, and as you achieve those, progress to bigger ones. But don't procrastinate too long.

4) **Keep the number of goals realistic.** By having a few specific goals that are also diversified as to length of time to accomplish, you will have a better chance of not losing your focus and becoming discouraged with all of them.

5) **Further define your goals by establishing a series of steps inside of each one.** You will see your progress and this will help keep you on track. By sensing accomplishment, you will be driven to continue. The good feeling will surface. Sometimes at work, I have felt overwhelmed by the projects in front of me or deadlines to be met. I always take a moment when this feeling occurs to stop and re-goal set and break the problem down into manageable steps. Don't try to go from having only one thing done to having twenty things done in one step.

6. **Take a serious look regarding with whom you are sharing your goals.** Ideally you will have several projects going on at once. However, some of those should not be shared with anybody. This is to avoid the negative or pessimistic people who will either laugh at you or tell you "it can't be done." Forget them. Then there are goals that you should share, with your family perhaps. Or ones that should be only shared with a very close friend. Your game, you decide. Sometimes it's nice to share a goal *after* you have achieved it.

DREAMS & GOALS

TO ACHIEVE YOUR GOALS CONSIDER THE FOLLOWING:

1) **Remember what reporters use to write a news story: Who, what, where, when, why and how. WHO**—Who are the players in your game, and what roles do they play in achieving the goal. **WHAT**—Specifically, what do you want to accomplish. **WHERE**—Where do you need to be, such as at a specific job, or self-employed, at a training seminar, a Bible study, etc. **WHEN**—Establish time frames for your end result and also the steps along the way. **WHY**—Maybe the most important is why you want to achieve this goal. What are the benefits? **How**—What resources do you need? In what ways do you make progress?

2) **Make your goals realistic.** That doesn't mean setting your goals so low that they won't provide you with a sense of great accomplishment. Goals must stretch you, and you must be able to work and sacrifice to get them done.

3) **Make it something you can feel with your senses.** For example, if you can see it, you will be more apt to strive for the goal. Even a bank balance can be "seen."

4) **Make goals attainable/reachable.** As you progress through the steps needed to reach the end, you will no doubt be learning better and more ways to make the next step a reality.

5) **Finally, make it measurable.** Measure progress along the way. If your goal is to save $100,000, plan to strive to reach it in increments (of $10,000 for example). And celebrate those successes in a small way that will give you a sense of accomplishment. Savor the moment and then move on to the next level.

Overnight Success

Success doesn't usually happen overnight, or even in a short time period. Yes, you could become wealthy financially instantly if you inherit money or win the lottery. So few win the lottery that it really isn't a possibility. Success with getting an education, saving for retirement, learning a skill, etc. takes an investment of both time and energy. It isn't given instantly. Furthermore, success and satisfaction depends on how people fulfill their aspirations.

I am a pianist. Not the best by any means, but with some "brush up" practice, I can play for church and a wedding once in a while. I never play for money, as it is a hobby and an enjoyment and a gift to others. Besides, if you play professionally, you are expected to be good at it. But, back to the subject, I did not learn to play the instrument overnight. It took a lot of time, energy, willpower, getting over frustrations, and yes some God-given talent. It took perseverance. I didn't always like to practice, but one thing, it did get me out of the farm hayfield in the summer for an hour on Wednesdays to go to my lesson. Boy, did I ever look forward to that break—in air conditioning! With sacrifice, the effort "paid off" and now it is a joy. The same goes with saving and investing. Work for it and it will work for you.

Path of Least Resistance

Let's get straight to the point. You will not find what you are looking for on the path of least resistance. It is too well traveled. Take the high road. Do what it seems others are not willing to do. This may be as simple as packing your lunch. If you do this wisely you can increase your nutritional value immensely over eating fast food. Or bumping your 401(k) contributions up from 5% to 10%, maybe from 10% to 15%. It may be to car pool. You can save $50

DREAMS & GOALS

to $100 a month in gas if you do that. More ideas are covered in Chapter Seven, the chapter on tips or "Plays to Execute."

Remove Yourself

I am putting this in here to provide the inspiration or desire necessary to accomplish all of your goals. I know it is a very difficult thing to remove yourself from the daily grind of life to make such necessary changes, but you must. You must make the changes you know you have to in order to succeed. I was told once that the problem with life is that it is so "daily." That is so true. We all get so caught up in our daily routines that we do not do what it takes to get on the track to where we really want to go. I also once heard from someone very close to me that they were too busy trying to make a living, and that they could not make any money. That means they were caught in the rut of just paying the bills, and that they were not getting ahead. Maybe they were so caught up in it that they could not finish the training to get the better paying job. At the very least, they are caught up in their lifestyle, not on top of it. With knowledge, such as from this book, they could find ways to break out of the helpless cycle and find the causes for their lack of ability to save or get ahead.

Removing yourself from this daily routine will break you out of it. Remove yourself by getting away. I have been fortunate enough to have traveled to various places. Most have been here in the USA, but some were not.

You can find the inspiration you need by getting away. For me, it is one of the finer things in life. Get away to a nice hotel. I have enjoyed the amenities of luxury hotels on both US coasts. You can lay by the pool, away from your normal routine and plan, think, and draw out what changes you need to do to move to the next level.

That is where a honeymoon for newly-weds comes in. They get away. They enjoy themselves. They plan their future.

I say to all of you, and you know who you are: take that honeymoon now.

I know I told you to be responsible, and that might have meant to do what it takes to pay your bills and get back to work, but if you have not taken that first honeymoon, plan it now and go. The same holds true for all of you who have not taken that second honeymoon. Go! Do it!

DREAMS & GOALS

CHAPTER FIVE
Game On! Do it.

Pay attention. This game is real and you are playing it right now. So easy to say, but might be hard to realize. You must get going. The chapters that follow can guide you with strategies and tips but you must get started. Set up a spending plan. Once you do it, it will feel good because you will know where you stand on a daily, monthly, yearly basis. When you spend over your limit you will be able to calculate the effect. When you spend less than you make you can calculate the gain. You need a hard and fast guideline to follow, and it definitely *starts* with tracking your expenses. First, know where your money goes. It may surprise you. And if it does—good—because that puts you on a learning curve of power. Knowledge is power. You will be so much more in control from that point forward.

Habits

We are all creatures of habit. They can be either good or bad. Habits include patterns related to health, daily living, driving, entertainment, and spending. Get into a pattern of good habits. This will improve not only your physical and mental health, but your financial health as well.

Snuff-out Smoking

This one is a big one. Fortunately, neither of us has been addicted to nicotine, but we have seen firsthand what it does to others. Realize that not only are you diminishing your precious health, but literally burning up your finances. At one $7 pack per day, you will spend $2,555 per year! Plus there is potential for higher insurance premiums not to mention doctor bills. Why is this still seen as "cool"? It is hard to understand why intelligent folks will spend hard earned money to ruin their health and financial situations, shorten their lives, and just plain smell rotten in the process. There was a person working at the office years ago that told me that he and his wife spent $4,000 that year in cigarettes. I about choked. Not until that time did I realize just how much people can spend on a bad habit. At that time, you could put $2,000 in an IRA fund, so they both could have funded their IRA—*just on cigarette money alone*—by cutting the habit. Wow! Just do that for a few years and you will enjoy a nice little nest egg later.

Drugs

What can we say here except illegal, expensive, destructive, and for lack of a better word—dumb.

Drinking

See smoking above. Consistent and continual dollars spent on drinking will have a significant, negative impact on savings for your future retirement.

Goals

We have addressed defining and setting goals in a previous chapter. But for discussion here, goals can be considered a habit. To win at the game, you are required to set goals and make a good habit of continuing to focus on them. Follow a plan of assessing where you are on each one. First, define and set your goals. Second, periodically assess each step you are taking or have taken down the path of achieving those goals. Third, make adjustments to each of those so that you don't veer off the course you have set for yourself.

In summary, allow yourself to have a good habit of monitoring your progress. You must set your own mind to do this often; even daily may be required. There is an old joke that goes something like this: "His mind is like concrete, all mixed up and firmly set." Yes, this can work both ways, either for the good or bad, but if you have that mindset working towards good things and goals, we don't see that as a problem as long as you are within the law, following good moral standards, and not hurting anyone else. Regarding financial goals, some things will come quickly, and some will require a long period of time. But the habit of persistence is like the concept of the turtle and the hare. Most often patience will win the race (the game) every time. It is back to plain old discipline. You must develop good savings habits to win.

Short Term/Long Term

One of our former bosses was fond of frequently saying, "Short term pain, long term gain." He not only meant making a profit in business, but improving yourself as a person as well. It is easy to understand this as reality, but sometimes it is hard to put this principle into practice. People don't always want to get up and go to work every day. We often shun the idea that daily exercise is good for us. We sometimes cannot help but eat that second helping. Others struggle with breaking an addiction. But, we must develop a mental state that tells us internally that we must sometimes do the things that we perceive as hard to do, at least at the time. Therefore, doing something that we don't want to do, or breaking a bad habit—is short-term pain—but the long-term results will be good. We will feel better about ourselves and meet our goals if we stretch to overcome the unpleasant issues.

GAME ON!
DO IT.

Mad Money

I cannot tell you where I learned the term (or the idea) behind the concept of what we are calling "Mad Money." This concept allows you to have a set amount of funds that you don't have to be accountable for to spend as you wish. It should be a category in your spending plan. It could be a set dollar amount, or a very small percentage of your disposable income, or perhaps, miscellaneous amounts from other sources of income outside of your normal job or investment income.

Setting up this amount will be a source of a sense of freedom and will most likely help keep you from overspending. An analogy that comes to mind is like someone being on a diet that just happens to like chocolate cake. Let yourself enjoy a piece of cake once in a while, just don't eat a whole cake every day. Likewise, spend a few dollars now and then without feeling guilty. Just don't go hog wild.

My sisters and I routinely comment and laugh about some of our purchases. We always say, "Yes, but it came out of my 'mad money' account." And, lo and behold, generally it is something we bought at a garage sale, a flea market, antique shop, or at a dollar type store. This reminds me of an incident several years ago, when I bought a really nice, name-brand sweatshirt at a garage sale. It is still in style, and I have received many compliments on it. I can still hear my sister saying, "Yes, I had to push you into buying it." It was 25 cents! My nephew, who doesn't seem to enjoy saving like the rest of us, saw it and exclaimed, "That is a really cool sweatshirt!" I smiled and replied, "Yes, I got it at a garage sale, and the funds to purchase it came out of my 'mad money' fund." Stingy? No. Frugal? Yes. Wise? Definitely.

Remember, play the game not only to win, but also to enjoy it along the way. Savor the moments.

Motivators

What motivates you? What gets you out of bed in the morning? Why do you do the things you do? What are your motivating factors? Obviously, by purchasing and reading this book, something is telling you that you have a desire to gain some kind of knowledge to improve your life.

We all have different personalities, and that is a grand thing. I tell one of my pals that I'm glad that he isn't just like me; if he was I couldn't stand him. Can you imagine if everyone drove the same model and color of automobile? That would be a great disaster because confusion would be rampant. Different personalities are crucial to the world. We must accept that people are different and learn to work and live with them. Of course, we are wise not to hang out with the "wrong crowd." We all have different things that motivate us. We are writing here about accepting ideas that will move you to make changes in your life, not only to gain financial wealth, but also to garner more general happiness, have better relationships, possess a growing faith, and maintain better health. In short, become wealthy.

Everyone is motivated by different things and in different ways. Embrace that thought! You must define what you are trying to accomplish and allow yourself (possibly force yourself) to be motivated in whatever way works for you. Think about who you are trying to impress. We maintain that you must impress yourself first, and that most people (outside of your family and true friends) couldn't really care less about what you do or have. Don't think of this as conceit. You must be happy with yourself first before you can help others and treat them fairly and with respect.

GAME ON!
DO IT.

CHAPTER SIX
Game Time Strategies

Now that you are aware of and have begun to master the fundamentals, and realize that the game is on, you can now implement the various strategies of your choice in order to win the game as you define it. We suggest the following strategies, but you can create some of your own along the way also.

Quality vs. Quantity

How much stuff do you really need to buy? Sometimes buying quality is much more important than buying excess quantities. For items that you plan to keep and use for a long time, quality counts. Examples are tools, furniture, classic clothing, appliances, and even smaller items such as home exterior paint.

My dad did not buy a lot of tools, but when he did he bought the best. For example, almost 45 years ago, he bought a new chain saw. At the time it was top of the line for its class size. Over the years we cut brush and trees at the ranch and a lot of firewood. Yes, we replaced chains, pull start rope, spark plugs, filters, etc., but to this day that little engine still runs great and has never been apart for repairs. Quality plus maintenance, every time.

Read the Fine Print

The saying goes, "The big print giveth and the small print taketh away." Take this saying to heart and never forget it. This is like, "If it appears too good to be true, it probably is." Of course, there are exceptions to every rule, but beware. In today's world, it seems, unfortunately, the trend is to "get the best of" someone else. Although we advocate making a good living, it should be done honestly.

Read everything, and understand it before you sign on the dotted line. If you don't, you can lose financially. Ask a lot of questions and have them fully explained to your satisfaction. If they aren't, ask someone else to explain, there are experts in every field. Use the Internet. It's easy and is very inexpensive (or free at the library).

We've all experienced emotional buying and also buyer's remorse. Buying on emotions can cause you to wish you hadn't at a later time. Do your homework, and think about your decisions. My Dad never bought anything major without "sleeping on it overnight." Sure, there may have been a deal or two that got away over the years, but overall, I know it saved him from doing the wrong thing in many cases.

When I was in my teenage years, there was a grandmotherly figure at church that gave me some advice one day. The subject at the moment wasn't a financial matter, but it applies to that also. She said, "If in doubt, don't; if no doubt, do." Wise words. Just do your homework, ask for advice, and follow your heart.

Ask for Help

We all have to ask someone else for expert advise at times. I know of NO ONE who is a doctor, lawyer, accountant, mechanic, plumber, veterinarian, teacher, farmer, etc., all rolled into one person. You may be an expert in whatever you do, and all jobs are important. But you cannot know everything. Therefore, when you need help or advice, seek it out. Sometimes you can get information for free, and sometimes you must pay for it. Whatever the case, if you *need* information about anything, get the information you need *before* you make decisions. Do your homework when it comes to financial matters and ask advice. It will serve you well in the long term.

You Cannot Spend Your Way to Wealth

Years ago, when I worked for an accounting firm, there were some clients that just fascinated me. One was an older couple that had worked hard for their money and saved and invested it well. You would never know by looking at them how large their financial asset net worth really was. They weren't misers, but they didn't flaunt their wealth either. They wore average clothing, but looked clean and sharp. They drove a larger car, but not top of the line. They lived in a modest neighborhood. And they knew where every penny was spent, and expected us to keep track of it. And, even more impressive, they gave away a lot of money to many charities. She once told me they were able to do that because they saved, invested, never chased overnight success, or fell for get rich quick schemes. She also said, "You cannot spend your way to wealth."

Then there was another client and his wife that appeared to have the world by the tail—the latest, fanciest suit; the new, flashy, luxury car; the jewelry, etc. And something else that they possessed—debt up to their eyeballs. They were constantly worrying about how to make the next payment on several things. They did work hard, but they couldn't control their spending. I recently heard about them again, and it appears that they are still chasing that dream of spending big, and are nowhere near being able to retire comfortably. They were too into "lookie what I got," and no one was really impressed. The first clients described above really had "lookie what I got," and it included peace of mind, generosity, friends, and joy.

GAME TIME STRATEGIES

e first clients had learned that there was more to life than money and material things. Yes, they did have material things, but they did not let those things "own" them. We all need food, clothing, shelter, transportation, etc., but we must keep all things in perspective.

Planning

I've heard a saying about the rich and the poor. It goes something like this: Rich people plan ahead for many generations, and poor people plan ahead for Saturday night. Wow! Which category do you fit into? Think about it. Do you save and plan for retirement, buying a house, a more reliable car, college for yourself or your children, or do you just think about scraping enough money together to go out to a nice restaurant on Saturday night? Believe us, if you can really get your act together, save up money by watching your spending and managing your investments and debt, you will not have to worry so much about that meal out once in a while. It can be a treat and a joy if there is less worry involved. Time and again, we have said, save and plan now, you won't have to do so much later.

We all know rich people, and we know poor people. We aren't saying that the rich will always be rich or the poor will always be poor. Rich people can make mistakes, squander their wealth, or run into obstacles that will diminish their wealth. And poor people can and do dig themselves out of a financial hole, by working hard, getting an education and putting it to use, and saving and investing. They don't always try to keep up with the Joneses. The trick is to DO SOMETHING about improving your situation. Trial and error, patience, and perseverance are the keys. Make an attempt, and if you fail, make adjustments, then attempt again. You will find you learn and grow more by failing than by continuing on the same path.

Mistakes

Everyone makes mistakes. The old joke is, "I thought I was wrong once, but I was mistaken." There is no way to live a life without mistakes. The trick, however, is to learn something from every one of them.

You must adjust your game so as not to repeat the same mistakes over and over. A mistake can be a great learning opportunity and press you to adjust your methods and habits. It could turn out to be the best thing for you.

No one sets out to let goals of security and financial freedom fail. It just seems to happen. Many people make the same basic mistakes, such as lack of planning, being uneducated in how savings and insurance plans work, procrastination, and last, assuming that "someone else" will be responsible for their future, such as their broker, accountant, banker, insurance agent and most importantly, their government. We are showing you how to avoid these mistakes and how to get started now to make money work for you toward financial independence.

Basics

Some say that the average person is not smart enough to make intelligent decisions about all of the options available for becoming financially independent. Horse feathers! We claim that financial institutions, the government, and Wall Street, among others, have complicated simple business way beyond what it should be. People of average intelligence can understand financial issues if they get all of the facts. There are lots of options available that can minimize your taxes, give you more disposable income, help you save money and also make good choices when investing that can make you financially secure and wealthy.

GAME TIME STRATEGIES

What you need is a plan, specifically a Spending Plan discussed later in this chapter. Experience will show you that planning for your future is nothing but simple mathematics. The keys to financial independence are not necessarily having a bunch of money, or being in the right place at the right time. Luck is not necessary, and you don't have to be a mathematical whiz. But you do need a plan. That is the first step to gaining control of your financial future. You must have a good road map to be able to reach your destination. It should be flexible, but firm, and you have got to stick with it!

If you stick to the basics, your planning won't be difficult. In the game you are playing, you must not vary from the fundamentals to get to victory. You must outplay the average person to win. Fundamentals are very obvious. Do not spend your time looking for the latest "get rich quick" scheme. These very rarely work, and we put an emphasis on the word "rarely."

YOU MUST STICK TO THE FOLLOWING BASIC PRINCIPLES OF SAVING AND INVESTING (THESE ARE NOT ALL-INCLUSIVE):
1) **Start NOW.**
2) **Pay yourself first.**
3) **Use time to your advantage and be consistent and persistent.**
4) **Make savings a priority.**
5) **Develop a winning attitude for the game.**

Get Started Now

We've all heard, "There's too much month left at the end of the money." People think that they don't have any extra income to invest for their future, and just getting through today is bad enough. However, we maintain that whatever your income level is, you can find *some* money to save. You need to check your spending priorities. This thinking is nothing new, as overspending, inflation and the taxman have been around a long time. Even if you have above average income, you still can feel the sting of these items. Do not give up. If you're serious about building financial security, you can find ways to arrange your income and spending to free up some funds for saving.

Paying Yourself First

Paying yourself first is one of the most important strategies. This means putting your values, yourself and your family above all other demands for your money. No matter what, deposit a set amount each month into savings and investments. You will be amazed at how fast your money (your game points so to speak) will build if you invest even a small amount regularly, even at a modest and reasonable rate of return.

If you fall into the "average American" category, you spend money on things that you don't need. Or you don't manage the money that you do have. You just float along in the game, spending as the needs and wants arise. It will take you some time to develop a good managerial attitude about your spending habits, but you must get things under control to win. Take charge for yourself. The main purpose of a spending plan is to give yourself control of your own money. You decide on what will be spent and where you can save. This will give you a good feeling (that winning sense) and you are in control instead of your money controlling you.

You must control your priorities. If you want to achieve financial independence, you will probably have to make some sacrifices. Over time, you can have whatever you want; you just can't have everything. That is a rule in the game (and life) that we must all accept.

GAME TIME
STRATEGIES

To further the points regarding starting NOW and also paying yourself first, just look at the current facts about retired people in America. Most people fail to accumulate enough funds to retire with any sort of comfort. They are depending on Social Security to make up a big portion of the shortfall. However, retirement income from that source is dwindling and is expected to make further declines. **Do not rely on Social Security to provide you with an adequate retirement.** It was designed to be a supplement, not a complete source of retirement funds. You are responsible for making sure that you have enough to support yourself with dignity when you are at retirement age. You will earn a lot of money over your working career. For example, if you make just $25,000 per year over the 40 years we consider your working career, you will have earned *one million dollars.* Isn't that amazing? It turns out it is not so much about how much you make, but how much you keep and allow to let grow, that really matters in the long run. Again, it is how you manage your expenditures and your savings that will determine if you are financially secure in the way you want to be. You must act now, or in a few years you will be in the same position that you are in now, with a big exception—you will have less time to make up for shortfalls.

Put your "pay yourself first" funds into an investment plan and consider that your "NEVER TO BE TOUCHED" fund. And by that we mean—don't touch until the goal is met, and then it can be used for its intended and planned purpose. The decision here is, "I've been overspending, there's been nothing left, so now I'm paying myself first." So start paying yourself first, into the "NEVER TO BE TOUCHED" fund. Make the decision, make it irreversible, set the terms of use for the fund, and live up to the terms. Even if you are already in a mud hole, this will help you get out and get on top and gain financial success.

Eventually, this fund will allow you to make a major purchase such as buying a home, or to build retirement investments. You must define the amount or percentage that you save, so that you can reach your long-term goals, but we would suggest a minimum of 10% of your income. This may be hard to do at first, but it will need to be increased as time goes on and situations allow to really build your nest egg. Important—get started! Get a mindset that it truly is "untouchable." If you take money out of this fund, it will definitely put the realization of your goal further down the road of time.

One of our dads always said, "Work hard for your money, save some, and later it will work hard for you." We have addressed the amazing power of compounding and the Rule of 72 in a previous chapter. But for now, consider that your savings are like employees. Like being the owner of a business, do not let those employees sit around and do nothing. Let your funds work for your future.

Time and Consistency

With time and consistency, you can reach your goals. You must have discipline to save and it is imperative to start as early as possible. Time is one of the most important factors in your financial plan. It does not take a lot of money to build independence and/or meet your goals if you begin early enough.

Priority

Again, you must set your priorities. Sit down and really think about what those are. We have mentioned that a goal is to truly become wealthy, and that wealth is not necessarily defined by a large bank account or lots of material things. It encompasses having friends, finding joy, obtaining bits of happiness here and there, and a general sense of well being. Make enjoying life a priority; only you can define what it is that makes you happy. You are the one to turn your life in the direction to make it go the way you want it to go. No doubt, there will be outside influences that will pull at your steering wheel so to speak, but you must keep your hands on that wheel and constantly make adjustments. Just like a pilot flying from coast to coast, lots of factors come into play, such as the winds and weather, and inputs are needed to keep on course. Do not be afraid to make adjustments.

Seek a desire to get on track to where you want to go. Ask for divine guidance to find your game, your track, your goal, whatever you wish to call it. Keep telling yourself to stay motivated, however hard that might be at times. Remember back to the turtle and the hare story. Be consistent and persistent. There is no shame in forging ahead in small steps, but just keep playing the game!

Winning Attitude

Success. You are playing a game, and your goal is to gain success, which must be defined by you. You must have an attitude that you expect to succeed. If you don't, you will wind up in the end where you expected in the back of your mind all along. With hard work, you can develop an attitude of enthusiasm, excitement, being positive, and confidence for what you are doing and planning on achieving. You must have a desire to win, and a desire to not give up. Whatever you think you can or cannot do, it turns out that you are exactly right! Do not accept being poor, unhappy, or just plain "run of the mill." A winner of the game will stay motivated as long as it takes to win. Most people can stay motivated for at least a short time, but as more time is sometimes needed, the fewer percentage of people can and will stay the course.

You must learn to see yourself as free, happy, successful, and financially independent. If you think it will happen, success stands a much greater chance. Your expectations of yourself will be more important than what anyone else thinks about you and your actions. Don't put off saving and investing until tomorrow. In life, you will get what you demand, sacrifice, and work hard for. Many people do not put off until tomorrow the things that they cannot afford today, and as a result they become debt-laden. This happens because their spending desires for today are stronger than their desires to win the long-term game. If your goal is to be average and ordinary, then fine, it is your choice. If not, then play the game to be a bigger winner.

Despite all of the negative things that happen, we still are blessed to live in the United States of America. We have freedom, a capitalistic economic system, and freedom of faith. You can achieve lofty goals and realize dreams here. Other than God's love and gift of salvation, if you believe and accept, nothing is free. Sacrifices and hard work are required. A winning attitude cannot be purchased. It is not for sale. You cannot go to college and get a diploma that says you now have it. Your attitude will be the difference in everything that you do. Set your goals high, put a little bit of a "dreaming" attitude with that, and you will be successful.

Excuses

It seems like it is always convenient and easy to come up with an excuse not to act. Examples are, "I don't have any money," or, "I don't have the time," or, "I cannot change my habits," or, "The world is against me." The list goes on. But, you are in control

GAME TIME STRATEGIES

of your game, and you have the ability to start this very minute to take more control of what you are doing in life. You can plan, educate yourself, start with a first step, and develop the winning attitude. Winners of the game have something in common and that is that they stay motivated to reach their goals. When the "excuse demon" pops into your head, fight back by remembering that this is a long-term game (battle if you will). Remember that all journeys are one step at a time. Keep on track; ask for help, pray about it, whatever it takes to keep moving forward. You can do it!

Dollars vs. Nickels

My brother-in-law always says that too many people step over dollars to pick up nickels.

As we have said, the focus of this book is about playing a game to be wealthy through your actions, especially saving. It is not about earnings. For this portion, we are assuming that you are earning to your potential. What is meant by the saying is, be sure that you address the large savings potential areas first, and then move on to small areas.

For example, curb your tendency to spend $100 at the mall on new clothes every weekend before you tackle cutting a few coupons to save $5 at the grocery store each week. If you have written out your spending plan as outlined later in this chapter or in another section of this book, you will know where your big expense categories are.

Another saying is "take care of the nickels and the dollars will take care of themselves." This relates to saving, saving early, and letting your funds grow through time via compounding. This is very powerful. Watch your spending and your financial lifestyle will be improved greatly.

Stingy vs. Frugal

Where do we draw the line? How far should we go to save money? As we keep saying, there should be a balance to everything. We believe you must save and plan, not only for a healthy financial life now, but for the future also. But, a healthy financial plan includes enjoying some money now—in a sense—being wealthy, and happy with what you have and are able to do. So—being frugal leaves no room for being stingy.

Of course, some would see each situation differently from other people regarding this subject. What we think might be frugal, you might see as stingy. However, we believe that the difference is in the way you treat others or are seen by others. For example, if you choose not to eat a meal out, you might be frugal, but if you stiff the waitress the tip, you are stingy. If you carpool to work, you are frugal, if you shortchange your share of trips or gas funds, you are stingy. Therefore, strive to be frugal and wise with your funds but draw the line when it comes to being stingy. We know of no one who is truly stingy that is truly happy.

Guide your behavior with a set of internal priorities that supports frugality, if you must. Remember, you are playing a game to gain true wealth. All of those spending whims that don't match your goals will become a struggle and you will not be satisfied when you give in to those temptations and ultimately don't reach your goals.

Most Americans behave in this way: spend everything (and more recently, more) that they can get their hands on. Time to revisit frugality. You must not fall into this trap if you want to be wealthy. Most people save almost nothing of their disposable income. You must develop a financial strategy—the game plan and rules.

LET'S REITERATE SOME RULES AND STRATEGIES:

1) **Don't deprive yourself.** You must allow yourself some fun or discouragement will set in. Set an amount in your spending plan for a hobby, time out with friends, an addition to your wardrobe, etc. See the discussion in the "Mad Money" section. This is being frugal, and is OK. Just don't be stingy and, for example, fail to occasionally enjoy a meal or a movie out with a friend.

2) **Don't go into debt.** Make debt your enemy, or at least most of the time. There may be situations where it is wise, such as a mortgage at a good interest rate on a needed home that has potential for appreciation, or a low rate student loan that will boost your earning power. What we are talking about here is interest on credit cards for items that immediately depreciate or are luxury items. In other words, your wants, not your needs. Being debt free will allow you to save your money for what you really want or need. Being debt free will keep the Rule of 72 working for you, not against you. Remember, it only takes a credit card company a few years at high interest rates to make you pay double for everything you buy on the cards. They double their money, and it comes out of your pocket, and therefore, out of your savings.

3) **Money is for living.** *Living modestly will allow you to raise your standard of living.* How simple is that? That is one rule of the game that eludes most people. You must save and spend your money wisely to be able to raise your

standard of living. Get this in your head. You don't have to make more money to raise your standard of living, it's about how you spend and save which ultimately determines how well you will live.

4) **Don't fall into spending traps.** Again—be frugal. If you tend to spend a lot of money at the mall on "stuff," stay away from the mall! You aren't being stingy by not letting yourself get caught in these situations. Don't read advertisements just for entertainment, or you will get sucked into them and entertain yourself by buying the items in the advertisements. Ads are powerful. These people are masters at enticing you to change your actions (spending more). The biggest trap—50% off or more— look how much you are saving—but guess what—you are not saving—you are spending—on things you didn't "need" until you saw the ad—they are playing on what emotion inside of you? GREED. They are making you greedy by wanting to buy something for less (supposedly) than it's worth—such a good deal—not—not a good deal—a total loss. Wow—did you get taken. Garages are full all over America—with this "stuff."

Don't let little setbacks keep you from winning by getting off track or becoming discouraged. We are all human and fall into temptation. Learn from your mistakes. Look back, right now, at some purchase you made just because the sale or special price looked so great. OK, it's over. Just continue to think in terms of long-term goals and the winning of the game when you get tempted to buy things you don't really need.

GAME TIME
STRATEGIES

Spending Plan Vs. Budget

Budget. In general, the word means *an estimated cost of living*. What does that word mean to you? To most, it means a restriction on spending, being limited, having no fun. I do not agree with the concept of "budgeting." Surprised? However, I do agree with having a spending plan, as I believe it is different than a budget. A budget is a perceived license to spend all of the money allocated to (earmarked for) a particular category. A spending plan better defines your goals, hence the word "plan." A plan will help keep you from wasting money. It will put you in control. You can be on the road to figuring out how you want to spend, and a plan gives you choices.

Everyone, with the exception of those who have so much money that it doesn't matter anyway, should have a plan. The less you have translates into the more you need a plan. Your plan can be very detailed or a simple, general plan. You get to decide how detailed it is. This is how you make your money do what you need it to do for you and want it to do for you. Write it down, and be specific with your goals.

THERE ARE MANY REASONS TO HAVE A SPENDING PLAN. A FEW OF THEM ARE AS FOLLOWS:

- **To determine where the money goes.** Most people do not know all the places where they spend their money. Generally, they know where the big amounts go, but it is the little ones that trip them up.
- **To get out of the debt hole.**
- **To live within your means.**
- **To save for big, upcoming expenses, such as a new home or college.**

- **To save for unexpected expenses or a job loss.**
- **To be able to buy the things you want or need.**
- **To be able to save and invest.**

This is not a complete list, but you get the idea. Having a spending plan is not meant to lower your standard of living, in fact the opposite is true. Being in control will allow you to more wisely use your funds, no matter what the level is. Appropriate financial planning will take you from where you are at currently and only improve your financial condition from there.

DO NOT USE THE FOLLOWING EXCUSES FOR NOT PLANNING:

- **A spending plan will require too much time.** You will need to sit down and put some thought into the process. However, toiling more at work, stressing over finances, or arguing with a spouse about money all take plenty of time and energy too. More than if you have a well-developed and followed plan.
- **I don't want to be restricted.** You will be more restricted if you continue to waste money. Besides, a good plan allows for some fun spending, also.
- **I don't like figures.** Many people don't like arithmetic. However, your plan should not be difficult math. Keep it simple.
- **No one else I know has a plan.** That is not your problem. You are doing this to improve your situation, not theirs.
- **I'm too busy, too poor, too old, etc.** Everyone can make these excuses. Find a way around it.

We'll talk more about these issues a little later. Remember, you need to devise a system that will work for you. But first, back to the thinking concerning spending plans. Some people will plan for the

GAME TIME STRATEGIES

big, fixed expenses and use a cash system for the rest, for example, drawing out money from the ATM and only spending that amount each month. That may be a good idea, provided that you are limiting your expenses to what you really need, and a few wants thrown in. For example, if you normally spend a total of $1,000.00 per month on several selected spending categories, cutting that down to $800.00 may be a good idea. However, always spending the full $800.00 may not be the wise thing to do. It all comes back to discipline.

Develop Your Plan

The very first thing you must do in developing your plan is to determine where your money is going. So for at least a month, two or three is better, write down every penny that you spend every day, and put it in a category. Do this in a simple spiral notebook. Define categories such as gasoline, groceries, clothing, prescriptions, hobbies, etc. Use enough categories to give you a clear picture. Do not think that any expense is too small to note. Consider that just a couple of dollars a day is $730.00 per year. For example, if you go to a coffee shop and buy a $4.00 coffee every day, that's $1,460.00 per year. If you buy a drink and chips or a snack every day (not good for your health either) at the convenience store for $5.00, then that's $1,825.00 per year. Too much of any of this is over $100.00 per month. That's a lot. Writing it down every time you indulge in these *luxuries* will show you how often you do this and how much it is really costing you. Discover these and other areas where you can significantly reduce your spending. For example, if you just have to have something to drink or munch on during the daily drive or when you are buying gas, bring something with you from home! Plan for it, have a little cooler or coffee in one of those "stay hot" containers. Plan, have what you want, and pay a fraction of the cost.

Also, go through your checkbook and credit card statements and note all of the large expenses for the past six months. This will catch expenses that occur maybe twice a year such as a semi-annual auto insurance bill. This will also point out if your record keeping is up to par. Figure your average spending for one month. Now you know what you are spending money for. You are now less ignorant of your situation, and fears can be faced with greater clarity.

Next, make a chart of your monthly income (include all sources) and subtract taxes. Now compare this figure with your expenses. If you are spending more than you make, your spending plan will help solve this problem. We think that you will be amazed at what you are spending your money on. Pick an area or two to cut down on, don't try to cut out every non-essential thing at once or you will become discouraged, and like a fad diet, you will fail at it.

Next, decide on a couple of achievable goals, where you want to redirect your spending. These should be specific, such as "put $200.00 in my savings account," "pay an additional $100.00 on the credit card balance each month," or "brown bag to lunch two times per week." Make this a priority, and readjust your spending to make it happen. Move funds or take these steps first thing.

One goal that you should definitely set is to always pay more than the minimum amount due on credit cards or accounts. Even if it's just a dollar, or five, or rounding the minimum up to the next $10 or $50, doing this will not only pay down the balance faster, it reports to the credit agencies as "paid more than the minimum." This is much more positive on your report than just paying the minimum. And this can help when you need to have that house mortgage at a good rate.

GAME TIME
STRATEGIES

Now, build a worksheet for the month, using spending categories that you define on the left. Make a column for "spending plan" and one for "funds spent." A third column should be for the variance between the first two columns. You will be able to see where you have either over spent, or have made your goals. You could also do this by the week, in case you have trouble tracking it on a longer-term basis. Study your variances. To cut spending, reduce each category by a small amount, not cutting one thing out completely. Of course, some categories should have no variance, such as the mortgage or car payment. And remember, DO NOT completely cut out things that are fun and enjoyable. Remember, we are not advocating cutting your lifestyle so much that you become unhappy or discouraged.

You will have times where you overspend, such as for emergencies. Do not give up. Keep up the process, and over a short period of time, you will learn where your funds are going and how to better manage them. Resolve to do this for, say, three months. Looking too long term initially will discourage you. Plan to spend, and plan spending wisely.

	Spending Plan	Actual Spending				Total Actual	Variance
		WK 1	WK 2	WK 3	WK 4		
GROSS EARNINGS							
TAXES							
MORTGAGE/RENT							
UTILITIES							
Electric							
Gas							
Water							
Phone							
Cable							
Cell							
INSURANCE							
Home							
Renters							
Auto							
Life							
Health							
AUTO							
Payment							
Repairs							
Fuel							
CREDIT CARDS							
GROCERIES							
CLOTHING							
MEDICAL							
GIFTS							
ENTERTAINMENT							
MAD MONEY							
TOTAL							

GAME TIME
STRATEGIES

CHAPTER SEVEN
Plays to Execute

The more you save, the freer you become financially. Anyone at any level of income can put some money aside. You just have to make up your mind to do it. Your financial plan is grounded in two things: earning money and saving money. We have purposely designed this book around the game of savings, not earnings. There are many general things that you can do to save money for the things you need or want. Start saving today and you may start to live a thriftier life (at least temporarily), but perhaps it will be much "richer" in a sense. Remaining free from the tyranny of money is a feeling that most people do not accomplish. The following are several tips you can employ to help you cut some corners. Remember, the track star in his quest to win the game of crossing the finish line first will utilize the shortest distance around the track.

General

Avoid the Sunday Ads

There is a reason that half of the paper in the Sunday paper is made up of advertising—to make you part with your money. And, look at the main body of the paper also. A great percentage of each page is advertising. Ads must continue to help sell products, or retailers, vendors, and other companies would quit spending THEIR money on them. When you read all of those ads, you are setting yourself up to spend. Avoid the temptation: don't read them. One of our fathers had many sayings and one of them goes like this: "I want to buy, not be sold to." He rarely read advertisements, and when he did shop, it was what I called "on a mission." He never seemed to be tempted by anything except what he knew he NEEDED. You are the one that is in the driver's seat, so you decide what and when you want to purchase something. This is a very powerful position to put yourself into, and it is very satisfying. It is also important to buy the right quantity, even if a larger quantity is a better unit price bargain. Buy the amount you need and keep the rest of the money in your pocket. Always remember that advertising is a lure. It is designed to hook you like a fish. Once you get attached to it, you can't let go, so be very careful on how you view any type of advertising.

Recently, I received a small coupon booklet in the mail from a fast food chain restaurant. Looking at this set of coupons got me thinking about how they were attempting to get me to visit one of their establishments. Slick use of color, bold wording claiming "special deals," a statement of how much you could "save" by using the coupons inside, and the word "free" used so many times that it was mesmerizing. But a closer look at those coupons showed the true nature. Yes, you could get a "free" product by purchasing a combination of other products, but it left the second person without a complete meal. Guess what! You would have to spend more money at the regular price to get what you wanted. Let the buyer beware.

Auctions

Auction sales can be a source of entertainment, getting great deals, and of course people watching. However, be careful that you don't get caught up in the excitement of the moment and overbid on something, especially if it turns out to be an impulse buy. I have seen people buy things (tools quickly come to mind) at auctions that could be bought new at a lower price.

Bargain Hunting

Become a bargain hunter. Remember, it is your game, so turn this into a competitive sport. Who says you can't be aggressive in saving money and have some fun with it? Get a friend to join in the game and try to one-up the other in getting the best deal on something. Go shopping together with bargains in mind, and make impulse buying off limits. Remember, always for something that you NEED. Make your shopping about informed buying decisions. Buy wisely, not cheaply, as cheap can sometimes cost you in the end.

Watch "Bin" Merchandise

Those items on sale in big bins at the store usually are made up of outdated items or impulse-buy opportunities. Think twice before purchasing anything from those attention grabbers.

Buy in Bulk

This works especially well if you use a large amount of product. It makes economic sense to buy the larger product if is cheaper by the unit, and you will use all of the product. Consider splitting bulk products with neighbors.

Buy Off-Season

Anticipate your coming needs for the year. Some things, like clothing, get dumped at drastically reduced prices to allow for new inventory for the current or coming season. Examples include linens and wrapping paper in January, patio furniture and school

PLAYS TO EXECUTE
General

supplies in late summer, etc. Always be aware of advertised end-of-season sales, but as always, buyer beware; only purchase items if you are 100% sure you need them or will use them.

Take Care of It

You spend hard earned funds on lots of things. Take care of what you buy! I know of one person who bought a new pickup, and within one week there were soda spill stains on the seat and French fries ground into the carpet. Never mind the scratch in the fender from not being careful when parking in the garage next to the lawnmower. Be serious! Depreciation happens quickly enough without egging it on. This works for all durable goods including vehicles, clothing, tools, furniture, and electronics. Don't become wasteful by ruination. By that I mean ruining good merchandise that you paid good money for by damaging it foolishly. Growing up, if I broke something or let it get dirty, I had to help fix it or clean it. It became top of the mind to not be careless.

Change Your Mind

If you are in the checkout line and change your mind about making a purchase, do not be afraid to hand it to the clerk and politely say that you have changed your mind. It happens frequently and they will restock the shelf. Better to decide then and there rather than either waste money on an unwanted product or the time to return it later at customer service.

Dislike Clutter

It is the rare person that doesn't have a bunch of stuff laying around, stuck in closets, under the bed, along the walls in the garage, just everywhere. Why? It is our nature to collect more of that stuff. However, the more stuff you have stashed, the harder it becomes to find something when you need it. If you cannot find something, you will replace it. What happens? A "need" is created to take time and energy to go to the store for a replacement, and money is wasted. Yes, you will tend to find the item right after buying that replacement. Also, don't leave food preparation areas a mess. It becomes too tempting to go out and eat or order food in.

When de-cluttering, don't buy new storage containers or worse yet, rent a storage unit before assessing your true storage needs. Weed out things periodically so that you can see the things you have spent money on.

Coin Sorters

Don't use a coin sorter anywhere that charges a fee. Go to your bank where you have an account. Most of them will sort and count it for free, especially if you deposit it into your bank account.

Know Where Discount Stores Are

Make good use of discount stores. Visit all of them in your area and scout out the feasibility of saving money at each one.

Dollar Discount Stores

There are several nationwide chains currently that sell discounted merchandise sometimes for pennies on the dollar. They buy items from distributors in odd lots, items with nearing expiration dates, or in bulk from larger retailers and pass the savings on to you. There is a wide variety of name brands and also lesser known brands or store brands available. There isn't a guarantee that you will always find what you need, but overall, the availability is very reasonable. Obviously, some items will not have

PLAYS TO EXECUTE
General

(or need) an expiration date, but items such as food will. Just be aware of possible out of date items. Try shopping in one of these smaller stores. You will be amazed at how much merchandise they can pack into a small, efficient store space.

Educate Yourself

If you are well read and well versed on current prices, you will be able to spot a bargain when it pops up in front of you. This includes new, used or antique items. I once bought an antique oak teacher's desk from a co-worker who claimed she no longer had use for it (I think it was more that the person needed money quickly). I knew what it was worth, and even though it needed minor repair, you can bet I jumped at the chance to buy it. And to top it off, they delivered it to my home. It is worth at least fifteen times what I paid for it. It is still in use in my home office.

Watch Fad Purchases

Do you truly need that latest gizmo? Think back concerning all of the half-hour, paid advertisements you have seen on television. Pick a number. Would you really use all of those kitchen timesavers that you have been tempted to buy? As with anything, there are some truly neat, useful items that have withstood the test of time. Consult with friends before buying, as they may have tried it and not liked the product.

Shop Flea Markets and Thrift Stores

This is similar to garage sales. There are many of these stores, especially in larger cities, and they can have quality merchandise. Check them out, you will quickly learn which ones to frequent. Clothing, furniture, electronics, toys, craft items, glassware, the list is long.

Garage Sales

A plethora of bargains can be found at garage sales. But, buyer beware, just because it is there and at a cheap price does not make it a bargain if you do not need it, or if you will never use it. The theory remains the same as with new item purchases. There is a good feeling when you can pay pennies for something needed. It is fun and a good opportunity to share time with a friend or relative that likes to bargain hunt also. Keep in mind that lots of barely used items are available, and can even be incorporated into gifts, especially items such as craft supplies or antiques.

Determine How Long You Must Work for a Particular Item You Are Considering Purchasing

For example, if you make $30,000 per year that $100 outfit or toy will cost you almost 9 hours of work to pay for it. Consider if it is truly worth it. To further explain, take $30,000 less 25% estimated taxes for a total of $22,500, and divide by 2,000 hours normally worked per year. That equals $11.25 per hour. Divide the potential purchase price of $100 by 11.25 and you will get approximately 9. That is greater than one full day of working time!

Avoid Impulse Spending

Avoid spending money on the spur of the moment. Even little leaks in the best boat will sink it eventually. Be mindful of the times when you impulse buy and change your habits.

Sell Off Junk

Get rid of merchandise that you no longer have a need for. Garage sales work both ways. Use the money to fund a family

PLAYS TO EXECUTE
General

outing, for needed back to school supplies, to give to your favorite charity, or any number of other things. You just put your resources to a better use.

Look Around Your House

Try remixing outfits for a new look—or use existing supplies for crafts or gifts. And food stored somewhere in the back of the pantry or freezer—use it, don't waste it.

Lottery Tickets

Sure, there is a winner once in a while, but those people are so very few. The rest of the players are definitely losing. Remember, the lottery is a tax designed to fill the coffers of someone else, namely the government. OK, so you might argue that the monies might be used for public good, or to help keep other mandatory taxes lower. Just note that if you choose to play, you are choosing to lose on average. Also remember, casinos are built on people's losses, not winnings.

Shopping Malls

I stopped going to the mall as much when I discovered that I could buy anything there (not everything, but anything). It wasn't as important as it previously felt.

Negotiate

Who says this practice is only appropriate for a home or automobile purchase? Tell someone. If you need an item, tell people. I find it hard many times to know what to buy people for gifts such as birthdays. Better to tell and both be satisfied.

Try New Products

Potentially save money by buying a generic product that costs less than another brand. If it works well and suits your needs, you have found a way to compound your savings. If it does not, you have only lost a small amount as you are not forced to buy that product again. Try a smaller size first to cut down waste.

Watch Placement

More expensive (read profitable) merchandise is usually at eye level. Check the upper or lower shelves to see if there is a less expensive product that will fully meet your needs. The best example that comes to our minds is cereal at the grocery store. The most expensive is placed at eye level.

Unit Pricing

Check all unit pricing such as cost per ounce. But don't overbuy something just because it is a few pennies per ounce cheaper. Not all merchants have tags showing unit prices, and they purposely make figuring prices difficult, so you have to be savvy about unit costs. If you are not a math whiz, don't be ashamed to carry a small calculator. It is your money that you are trying to save.

Rebates

If you buy products that come with a mail-in rebate, do not forget to mail in the proper paperwork! Is it a hassle? Absolutely. But remember, the sellers are counting on you not taking the extra step to obtain your rebate, or not cashing the check when you do receive it. Don't let them win at the game. You can get good deals on items such as motor oils, garden chemicals and supplies, and electronics, but as always, you must take the initiative to complete the deal.

Keep Good Records

Included are prior year tax returns and bank statements, guarantee/warranty paperwork on appliances and auto repairs, birth certificates, immunization histories, wills/estate planning, lock boxes, insurance policies, investments, emergency contacts, and credit card statements. You get the idea. The list goes on and on. When you need some information, it is very handy to have. It not only saves time, but replacement costs.

Recycle

Here we don't mean putting garbage items in the recycle bins, but recycling items that would normally be thrown away into new uses. Examples would be using egg cartons or other cardboards for crafts, worn out clothing for rags, trading magazines with friends, etc.

Rent Rarely Used Items

You might have a need to transport a large group of people infrequently. Consider renting a van for a few days to cover that purpose. Or, go in with a friend to rent a lawn aerator or seeder in the fall. Specialty woodworking tools for a weekend project fall into this category also. It may appear to be expensive at first, but long term costs are significantly reduced.

Do Routine Maintenance

Routine maintenance can slash your risk of expensive future repairs. Learn to do simple tasks yourself such as changing furnace filters, fixing leaky faucets, and changing the oil in your vehicles. Consider purchasing a handyman book for everyday tips, or check online for basic instructions. Better yet, tap into a friend's knowledge and share tasks that each of you might know how to handle well. Learn to paint.

On Sale?

You don't necessarily need any item just because it happens to be on sale. The word "sale" is so overused that we are surprised it still invokes a "gotta have it" mentality in most consumers' minds. Keep a mental inventory of supplies that you have on hand at home or at your business, and don't overbuy. If you don't have it, there is no need to store it either. On the flip side, if you know it truly is a bargain, and you will use the product, buy it.

Watch "Sale" Items

Watch merchandise that *appears* to be on sale, such as at the end of counters, aisles, or with large price signs. Often, it's not on sale at all. A trap. Merchants have done their homework, hire personnel to set up attractive displays, and read advertising methods to make the most sales.

Share with Someone

There is no need for everyone on the block to have a garage or house full of items that can be shared with a trusted friend or neighbor. Tools and gardening equipment quickly come to mind. You might not want to loan out that expensive new do-dad tool until you get to know the new neighbor a little better, but with time you will know what to do.

Comparison Shop

While it may not be wise either for minimal savings or time to comparison shop on every item, you need to compare prices on many purchases. The higher the cost, the more money that you can save by comparing prices. Check current advertising and use consumer magazines or the Internet.

Consolidate Shopping Trips

Get into the habit of making the best use of your time and transportation. Know where stores are located, what times traffic is lower, and the route you can take to cut expenses.

PLAYS TO EXECUTE
General

Styles

Accept the fact that styles change. There will always be fads. You simply cannot keep up with everything. If you try to do this, you will constantly be spending money needlessly. I have recently heard that most people are trying to keep up with people they don't even like. You've heard the old saying "you can't keep up with the Joneses," and it is true. And furthermore the joke is, "I finally caught up with the Joneses and then they refinanced." Take this to heart. You can buy quality products that are not faddish and stay reasonably in fashion. Wearing plaid bell-bottom pants from the '70s is not recommended. Keep your self-esteem! One of the most exciting things to me about fashion is denim jeans. I love to wear jeans, I feel most comfortable in them. There are even special days set aside in some professional work environments where employees specifically are allowed to wear jeans. Now this is a fashion I can keep up with and can save money at the same time. It even gets more exciting. It seems that the more worn out a pair of jeans are, the more in fashion they become. I would say that when it comes to money, this is the type of fad you are looking for. It falls right in the line of drinking water. This is a healthy thing to do and is inexpensive.

Team Babysitting

If you have children of the age that require supervision, team up with neighbors or friends in the similar situation. This is a great idea for date nights with your spouse.

Wait Awhile

If it is not an emergency, or not in the normal cycle of your purchasing, wait a period of time, for example a week, before making a purchase. Many times, you will either forget about it or decide that it was not necessary.

Windfalls or Inheritances

We cannot stress the following enough! You MUST exercise extreme discipline if you suddenly come into a substantial windfall or inheritance. Of course, if you are already well off financially and have discipline, it will be easier to manage this issue. But, if you are not, beware of what you spend, as funds can be squandered faster than you realize. We are not advocating saving every penny of it, but you cannot say that you weren't warned.

Volunteer Work Trades

Share work with friends. Everyone has some talent that they can (and will be willing) to share. If you are a good plumber, offer some time in return for someone else's time that is a great carpenter, etc.

Watch Your Steps

Don't pass by things twice in stores. You will be tempted to buy more the longer you spend in the store and the more you see merchandise. Also, remember, the restrooms are typically located in the back of the store for the simple reason you must pass by more merchandise to get there and back.

Remember the Game

The game is sometimes won or lost before you even start. It is in your attitude. It is in your planning. It is in your practice (remember, practice does not make perfect, but perfect practice makes perfect). It is in your heart. It is how you overcome failings.

PLAYS TO EXECUTE
General

Automobile

No doubt you cannot miss the already high, and certainly coming in a matter of time, higher prices of fueling and maintaining your personal automobile. The media is currently full of stories, blaming higher demand, greedy oil companies, world population growth (especially in India and China), bigger, more powerful vehicles, and the list goes on and on. We grew up with muscle cars and they are truly a joy to drive. However, their fuel efficiency was not a selling point. In fact, I must admit that I have two of them myself, and they bring me much joy to own and to have the memories. However, I do not drive them on a daily basis. What are we to do to fight this major battle going on with something we feel very near to? Short of selling your personal transportation (commonly known as a source of "freedom" in the USA), or permanently keeping the key in the "off" position, and walking or bumming a ride everywhere, there are numerous things that you can do to minimize your expenses.

Buy a Used Car

Buying a previously owned vehicle can significantly cut ownership costs. The moment you drive a new car off the dealer's lot, it will lose value. This is known as "immediate depreciation." A used car will lose value also, but at a much slower rate. Buying a used car can also provide a way to drive the type of car that you might not be able to afford new. You will also pay less for insurance, license plates, and personal property taxes. There are many good used cars available, and can be obtained through a reputable dealer or online through ads on common Internet search sites. Research the history of the dealer if you intend to buy a used car from one, and inquire with friends about their experiences with that respective dealer before buying a used vehicle.

Also, check consumer magazines regarding the model that you are considering purchasing for average repair history requirements. Avoid vehicles brought in from other states (ask why someone is trying to get rid of it hundreds of miles away), or cars owned by rental agencies (they are never driven as carefully by a renter as opposed to an owner). If at all possible, have the car you are considering buying checked out by your local, trusted mechanic. You may have heard the saying "buying used is buying someone else's trouble." That can be true in some cases, but if you do your homework, and have it checked out, you have a greater chance of avoiding potential disasters.

Reading and following advice on spending a certain percentage of your income on a car is a trap. It is not OK, for example, to pay 20% of your income on car payments just because someone decided on that figure. You must determine your needs and to a lesser degree, your wants, and spend at that level. If at all possible, you should put the amount of the car payment away in savings for several months before you buy. Can you get along well without those funds? Remember, the cheapest car you will own is the one you own now.

One thing I have done over the past twenty years is purchase my vehicles from my father-in-law. This has taken a lot of the uncertainty out of the shape the vehicle would be in. I know very well how meticulous he maintains his cars. In fact, early on when first dating his daughter I was somewhat intimidated to go over to her house because I knew off chance that my oil might get checked by her grandfather while I was there. But just talking to friends and acquaintances about cars they have, and what you like, opens up avenues of who has what and who might be willing to make you a deal that is beneficial to the both of you.

In addition, in my state of residence, there is a family exemption for sales tax when a vehicle is purchased within the family. The few thousand dollars I have saved this way too have added up over time. Quite honestly however, and that is what the core of this book is about, is the fact that most people have no business buying a new car in their current financial condition. If one makes an honest evaluation of their circumstances, they may only have $3,000, $6,000, or $12,000 in their spending plan to buy a car. That is what you should stick to. Buy what you can afford. You will immediately get to "keep" or benefit from the savings and that can be rolled over to your next "drive."

Your current credit score may be spelling out the fact that you should not buy a new car at all. This is an opportunity to build up your credit rating by buying a used one on a short-term, one-year payment plan. Negotiate payments you can afford, make them on time, and get your credit back in shape.

The last vehicle I bought with credit was once again one from my father-in-law. I went down to my local credit union and asked how much they would lend me. The vehicle was three years old and in great shape. The credit union would finance $20,000 for up to 48 months. This was great, the truck had a high "loan" value, and since the purchase price was $15,000, I was reassured that I would not be "upside down" the day after the purchase. However, instead of borrowing all the credit union would lend, I put $5,000 down and borrowed $10,000. In addition, I set up a higher payment that would allow me to pay it off in 15 months. I must be honest, it was somewhat painful given my current spending plan, however, I knew I would feel great about having it paid off in such a short time. This was in January and I even paid it off early by the next January. It felt great. What an accomplishment.

I have also been on the other side of a bargain. My wife and I purchased a 1993 automobile and drove it 10 years. A friend of my wife was looking for a car for her daughter. They did not want to spend a lot and wanted to buy a good used car. We made them a deal on our car and it too was a great feeling to provide something to them that they appreciated and could use when first starting out. Quite honestly, we could have driven that car for another five years.

Pay Cash for that Used Car

If at all possible, save up for a vehicle purchase. It is an asset that depreciates, so buying on credit is not wise. You will also tend to spend less if you are paying with cash, and you will instinctively take better care of it. If you must finance, shop for the best possible interest rate (dealers are higher in general), and make sure that you can pay off the loan without penalty. You may not be able to pay cash at first for a new car but make it a goal in your life. You will feel so good when you can walk up and dictate some terms on such a big purchase. The first step is to save up as much for a car as you can. Find a bargain, buy used, and put yourself in a better position to pay cash for your next one.

Know What It Costs to Drive Your Car

A fun, eye-opening exercise is to calculate what it costs per year per mile to drive a car. Let's take a car someone is paying $250.00 a month for in payments, $50.00 a month for insurance, and another $50.00 per month for taxes and license fees. Let's assume 12,000 miles per year are driven, the cost of a gallon of gasoline is $4.00, and gas mileage is 15 miles per gallon. Recap: $3,000.00/year payments, $600.00/year insurance, $600.00/year licenses and taxes. 12,000 miles divided by 15 miles per gallon equals 800 gallons of gas times $4.00 per gallon for a total of $3,200.00, for a total cost of $7,600.00. Divide that total by 12,000 miles and you get a cost of $0.63 per mile. You could throw in there a certain cost for depreciation, which would also include deferred maintenance such as tires, etc, and the costs could put you up near $1.00 per mile. This may not sound like a lot but give it some thought. I am four miles from the nearest grocery store. If I needed a gallon of milk and purchased that alone, I would put 8 miles on my car at a cost of $8.00. Added to the cost of milk, I would spend approximately $11.00 for that gallon of milk. I do not make these trips. Growing up, we lived out in the country. There was a saying by my father, "It would be a trip to town." I hated that saying but it was usually enforced. We didn't waste those trips either, and it comes down to planning your expenses wisely.

Buy a Gas Saver

With fuel prices constantly on the rise, it makes economic sense to buy a vehicle that gets higher mileage. You will have specific needs when purchasing a car, and those should be kept in mind. However, fuel will be a significant expense and should be considered heavily. A bigger, more powerful engine may be fun, but does taking a second or two less to get to sixty miles per hour really make a difference? Only you can decide. Buying a hybrid seems to be the new rage, but be wary, the increased purchase costs and unproven future maintenance repair expenses can quickly negate any fuel savings. Bottom line: Buy no bigger than you regularly use.

Carpool

Obviously, your car will not be equal as the one that you are sharing a trip with, but by carpooling, you will save approximately 50% on fuel costs, and will have less maintenance requirements, and a lower risk of your vehicle being in an accident. Find someone (that you can tolerate!) and share expenses.

Change the Air Filter as Needed

An engine struggling to draw in air to mix with fuel will burn more of that fuel. Air filters are easily replaced, and you will be able to buy quality replacements at discount stores. Check the owner's manual for proper sizing, and instructions on changing. Many cars have more than one filter. Be sure to check and replace all of them as necessary.

Change the Oil Frequently

Dirty oil cuts fuel mileage and risks damaging your engine. Have you priced a new engine lately? You don't want to get caught in that trap. Use a quality oil and filter that meets the manufacturer's recommendation and change it at least as often as the mileage or time requirements as suggested. If you are mechanically minded, you can do this job yourself, or have a trusted friend help you for further savings. Just remember to dispose of used motor oil and filters properly. Many auto parts stores will take used motor oil free for recycling.

I am a driver that does not drive the "average" number of miles per year that studies tell us that are driven by the average American. I drive less. Therefore let's use 12,000 miles annually

PLAYS TO EXECUTE
Automobile

as our number for savings calculations, and that we will use 3,000 miles as the limit to drive before an oil change is needed. Over the last 26 years (my working career) I would have driven 312,000 miles. Divide that by 3,000 for a total of 104 oil changes. I recently saw a sign "Oil change, $24.95." I can buy oil and a filter for a total cost of approximately $12.00. That is a savings of $12.95 per change for a total savings of about $1,350. If you are in a 30% tax bracket, you would have to earn almost $2,000.00 to pay for this one expense item.

Change Spark Plugs

Today's automobiles can go much further between spark plug changes than when leaded fuel was being used, plus the quality of the materials has been improved. However, they do wear out, so have them changed as recommended. The old "tune-up" is outdated, but newer vehicles have more parts to wear out, including oxygen sensors. Changing those as required can significantly increase your fuel mileage.

Check the Belts and Hoses

These will last a long time, but when they fail, you can have major problems. Never mind being stranded somewhere, and the costs of towing, but you risk significant damage to the engine. Have a trusted mechanic give them a once over.

Check Fluid Levels

Frequently check all fluid levels. This includes oil, antifreeze, power steering, brake, and transmission fluids. Also, don't forget the washer fluid. It is not critical to your car, but can be critical to your safety. Buy quality fluids and keep the levels at manufacturer's recommendations. Keep good maintenance records, especially who did the work and when. This information will be useful if warranty work is needed. Years ago, when I replaced the exhaust system on my classic car, I kept those receipts as it was for a lifetime replacement warranty. A few years later, when the mufflers needed replacing, you can bet I had that receipt and got a set of brand new ones free. A good friend was astonished that I had that receipt, but definitely couldn't argue with free. Frugal? Yes, and wise as well.

Use the Cruise Control

Steady driving speeds can save you fuel costs. Unless you are driving in hilly terrain where the engine is constantly struggling to keep a set speed, this is a wise choice. My father was always trying to cut corners, so to speak, and I can still hear him say "keep your foot steady" when I was driving his vehicle. That was wisdom before the days of the modern cruise control.

Buy a Full Tank

Fill the gas tank completely when you can. This will save you time, and a trip to the station. You are going to use the fuel anyway, and when prices are generally going up, you will avoid the next hike in the price.

Buy Fuel at the Lowest Price

Usually this is at a convenience store, as they are known to sell fuel at breakeven or a slight loss. They want to get you into the store to buy sodas, candy, toys, everything else. So, only buy fuel there. Use your credit or debit card at the pump, so you won't be tempted to go into the store. Besides, you can track your spending better with credit card statements or your bank account statement that way. Glance at the prices at more than one filling station once in a while. If you see prices have gone up considerably, stop and fill at the next one if the prices have not been raised there yet, and you need say, more than half a tank. Check online for current gas prices in your neighborhood, or en route to your place of employment.

Buy Gas When There Are No Lines at the Pump

Most filling stations have peak times when it seems the whole neighborhood is there, waiting in line. Be mindful of those times, and avoid the wait. You'll spend less in fuel idling or moving up in line, and precious time is not wasted. Unless you would have to go well out of your way to go back to the station, or are "running on fumes," schedule your fill-ups and save.

Check Into a Gas Rebate Card

There are numerous vendors out there that offer this service. Just be mindful of any hidden fees or requirements that might negate your savings. Many grocery stores also sell fuel and use of their "preferred customer" card can save you several cents per gallon at every fill up. Check with the store manager about getting a card, generally they are free and can provide useful coupons via mail, geared toward your regular purchases.

Consume Less Gas

Obviously, the best way to save fuel is to drive less. It cannot be said more clearly.

Never Buy a Higher-Grade Gasoline than Required

The difference between fuel grades is usually 10 cents per gallon. If your car is designed to run on regular fuel, do so. You will not have increased mileage (translate savings) by burning a higher octane fuel. Higher octanes are designed to prevent engine knock generally in higher performance or higher powered engines. Check the owner's manual for recommendations.

Use Self-Service Gas Stations

While the full service station seems to be on its way out, unless you need some type of service, or there is a torrential rainstorm going on, pump the gas yourself. You usually can save several cents per gallon doing this instead of using full service.

Don't Idle Needlessly

What a waste. Stop and think about it just a moment. What fuel mileage are you getting when you are doing this? Zero. The average goes down, the costs go up. We are not advocating that you shut off the engine every time you stop, but we're guessing that you are guilty leaving it running when chatting with the neighbor in the driveway, waiting on the child to come out of the school building, at a long fast food drive thru line, or various other places. Keep the mindset to turn off the engine when it won't be needed for more than a minute. My father was extremely frugal. He developed a habit of turning the engine off before he put the shift lever in "Park." Frugal? Yes. But it was a mentality of saving everywhere possible, and carried over into his other savings including automobile expenses.

Check Your Insurance Coverage

If you own a car that is paid for and is several years old, consider dropping your comprehensive and collision damage coverage. The insurance premiums can quickly add up to more than you will ever be able to recover from an accident or natural disaster. It is possible to raise your deductible limits to help reduce costs. Be sure that you are financially prepared to absorb any losses or increased costs if you do drop coverages or go with raised deductibles. You will still need to carry liability coverage as required by law and to protect yourself from losses where you are deemed to be at fault. Also, consider combining automobile insurance coverage with your homeowners or renters policy. You can save up to 15% by using the same company.

Keep All of the Tires Properly Inflated

Studies continue to show that a large percentage of tires are inadequately inflated as necessary. Do you remember as a child riding your bicycle with low tires—you just didn't have time to stop and inflate with that little pump? It was much harder to pedal and you didn't get to where you wanted to go as fast as you would have liked. Well, it's the same thing with your car today. More effort is needed, and therefore more fuel is spent. Checking the pressure when you fill the tank will save you precious fuel dollars, let alone wear and tear on the tires and other driveline parts. Check the sidewalls of the tire to be inflated or the owner's manual to determine the correct pressure. Buy a quality tire gauge and use it frequently. Safety is always a concern, so don't over-inflate. A relative has one of those newer cars that have tire pressure sensors at each wheel. Her husband insists on having the pressure at above the manufacture's recommended level by a few pounds, and the dashboard message usually reads "check tire pressure." Use common sense, and be wise.

Use Public Transportation

If at all possible, use public transportation. This can significantly reduce your vehicle cost outlays, especially fuel, maintenance, tolls, and parking fees. Not all areas of the country have this service available, or it might not fit your required transportation schedules, but it is worth checking into.

Slow Down

This is related to the bicycle example regarding tire inflation. The faster you wanted to get somewhere, the more effort needed to be expended. Your energy levels were exhausted faster. Driving faster requires more fuel, mainly due to wind resistance. Keep the speed at a reasonable level (always within the speed limit) and you will cut your fuel usage considerably. Again, this habit saves on maintenance and those nasty little tickets the police like to hand out. Also, for most trips, the time savings just don't add up to much, never mind the lower stress you will feel not always in such a rush and watching for the police all the time.

Avoid Jackrabbit Starts and Panic Stops

Gunning it at every green light may be a favorite thing to do, but it will cost you every time. A gradual acceleration habit will save you precious fuel and again, excess wear on tires. Also, at the other end, speeding up to your stopping point and slamming on the breaks is a gas waster, and who wants to spend dollars getting new brake pads and rotors?

Unload Extra Weight

Put your vehicle on a diet. Less stuff being lugged around means weight savings, which immediately translates into fuel savings. Why do you leave the camping gear stowed in the trunk from November through March?

Wash the Car at Home

If at all possible, clean your vehicle at home. You will save money by doing this, especially over the full service, automatic washes. Obviously, this is a better plan in the spring, summer or

PLAYS TO EXECUTE
Automobile

fall, leaving the winter cleanings to the robo-wash. Keeping your car clean in winter is wise, especially if you live in areas where the roadways are treated with salt for icy conditions.

Clothing

We've all heard the saying about "Food, Clothing, and Shelter." Regarding clothing, we all need protection from the harshness of nature, whether it be heat, cold, pesky insects, the sun, or a barbed wire fence. Needless to say, our society also dictates the need for cover up, as some things just don't need to be seen by everyone! Clothing costs no doubt have been kept down due to the nature of cheap imported goods in the past several years. However, read and listen to the news and you will understand that transportation costs and other producing nations desire for increased standards of living, including clothing, will certainly drive prices upward. Again, the goal is to satisfy your needs without breaking the bank account.

Learn to Change Clothes

When you get home from work, shopping, church, etc., change out of your clothes into everyday clothes. This will save ruining clothing. For example, don't work in the garage and get dirty or greasy in the attire that you wore to work or the store.

Avoid the Dry Cleaners

Purchase clothing that does not have to be dry-cleaned. Learn to read the labels before purchasing garments to determine if they can be safely washed. Countless dollars can be saved by owning washable clothing, because it is an expensive process for dry cleaning, let alone the time and transportation costs to visit the cleaners. Of course, some items must be dry cleaned, such as business suits. We recognize that your job may require this, so go ahead and have it done as necessary. Be wise and avoid spilling things onto your dry-clean only items.

Hand-Me-Downs

Make good use of the hand-me-down process. There is no need to spend hard-earned money on new clothing if there are usable items already waiting. Check the fit, and encourage children to wear hand-me-downs. Need we mention garage sales and thrift shops? Good clothes can be picked up there for pennies compared to new. Bargain hunting can be very rewarding, and not just for the dollar savings. There is a sense of "look what I got almost free," and you can socialize with friends or family while doing it.

Hang Up Clothes

If space allows, hang clothing up to dry instead of running the dryer. This also will save energy, and will save wear and tear on the fabrics. If you have an outside line, the clothes will smell fresher.

Learn to Iron

Learn to press your clothes that require it. The dry-cleaners will do it for you, but remember, they are in it to make a profit. Set aside a time to do this chore, you will be surprised how quickly you can iron a dress shirt or blouse. Get a quality, lightweight iron that will make the job easier.

Learn to Mend

Learn to mend minor items on clothes, such as sewing on a button or fixing a hem. The life of clothing can be extended considerably by doing this. Grandma used to darn socks by putting a light bulb inside and carefully repairing holes with a needle and thread. That may be a little extreme now, as socks today wear evenly and just plain get thin and so the darning process is antiquated. Nevertheless, you can do many repairs.

Declare a Moratorium on New Purchases

We dare say that the average American has more clothing in their closet than they ever wear. Go ahead, look in your closet and we'll bet there are a few items that you haven't worn in years, and probably didn't wear much even back when you first purchased them. You spent hard earned money on those. It is possible to cut out or eliminate new purchases for a time. The challenge is to determine what that time length is and stick to it. If you truly have a need for new items, such as requirements for a new job, the toddler has outgrown his or her shoes, or it is winter and the only gloves you own have holes in them, by all means, buy what you need. It is the luxury purchases that will break the spending plan.

Entertainment

We all like to be entertained or entertain others. It helps us keep our senses, reduce stress, interact socially with friends or family, and gives a sense of purposeful living. It truly can be a luxury. History tells us that over the centuries, humans have always strived to be entertained. Entertainment has included everything from chariot races of long ago to the modern digital television age. Whatever it is, embrace it and enjoy it. Learn to spend wisely on it to get the most enjoyment, and you will have a good feeling. Do what creates the best value of entertainment for you, not the neighbors or co-workers.

Annual Passes

Buy annual passes if it makes economic sense. For example, if you and your family enjoy going to the zoo several times during the spring and summer, look into the price of purchasing annual passes for everyone. Almost always, you will have a hefty discount as opposed to buying an individual day pass.

Don't Buy "Celebrity Stuff"

Merchandise such as T-shirts sold at concerts just pads the celebrities' pockets. If you go to concerts, avoid all of the extras. Your date, friends, or family will already know that you went and had a good time. The person that you see on the street could not care less.

Community Events and Festivals

Take advantage of community-sponsored events. Where we live, there is an annual "river festival" each spring. There are numerous events including concerts over a period of nine days that you can attend for a minimal cost of a five-dollar button per attendee. Pick the events that you will enjoy and GO! Just be aware of high price food and merchandise vendors, and limit your spending at those merchants. Pack your own snacks and drinks.

Learn to Entertain Frugally

Learn to entertain family with reading together, or playing games together. It is fun, is low cost, and will build memories of sharing and bonding.

Group Discounts

Ask for group discounts to movies, concerts, plays, etc. Many times you can get a discount of several dollars for each ticket

PLAYS TO EXECUTE
Entertainment

when purchasing multiple tickets. The show will still be just as entertaining, and you will have funds left for other purposes.

Outdoor Entertainment

Fun awaits you by being outdoors and enjoying nature. Picnics, camping out in the backyard, etc. can be very inexpensive, rewarding times.

Internet

Most medium speed Internet connections (DSL) will provide you with the necessary speed, as to not get frustrated waiting on the computer to churn. And, remember to bundle Internet with your phone services.

Mail Order Movies

There are now several companies that allow movie rentals via mail. If you rent several movies per month, this can provide a great savings, plus you generally can keep it as long as you wish, before returning and making your next selection. Plus, there is no spending time and precious gasoline on the trip to the video store.

Movie Madness

When you plan to go to a movie now, expect to pay higher prices not only for the ticket, but at the concession stand also. Theaters are raising prices of food items to keep their profits higher, in an attempt to keep the prices of tickets lower. If you enjoy going to the theater, keep your movie entertainment costs as low as possible with the following tips:

- If your schedule allows, such as when on vacation, or if you work a non-standard shift, you can save money by **attending movies during the day**. The movie will still be the same as it will be at the pricier evening showing.

- **Go at off times to avoid the premium ticket price**, if your theater charges extra, such as on Friday and Saturday nights.
- **Some theaters offer free showings of family movies, at selected times.** They usually are not first run productions, but your small child may not have seen the movie and will be thrilled for a time spent with mom or dad going on a "date." Also, watch for free tickets, such as when you purchase a set amount of groceries at your local store.
- **Go to the drive-in.** Yes, there are still a few drive-in theaters across the country. If there is one close to you, take advantage. They do show new releases and typically do double features, for a lower cost than one ticket at a regular theater. Some also offer no charge for children (age limit depending on the theater) or bargains for per-car pricing. Gather the friends!
- **Check out the discount theaters.** If you can wait six weeks or so after the initial first run of a movie, go to the "second run" theater. Movie prices currently in our town are $2.50.
- **Obtain coupons from a local entertainment coupon book.** They typically have ticket coupons for half-price.
- **Buy tickets in bulk.** If you go frequently, buy a book of ticket coupons and receive several dollars off of your individual purchases. Beware, make sure that the coupons don't have an expiration date.
- **Don't buy advance tickets online.** Avoid the typical $1 surcharge.

PLAYS TO EXECUTE
Entertainment

- **Eat before you go.**
- **Buy the large size popcorn and share with your companion.**

Serve Hors d'Oeuvres at Parties

Serve these at parties, not full meals. It is definitely cheaper, and your guests will have variety and will think it is great. This provides for a more relaxed, casual atmosphere, and isn't that what you want at your special party?

Share Media

Like sharing a magazine, share other items such as music CDs with a friend or family member that shares your same tastes.

Regarding Restaurants

Restaurant dining can become very expensive, especially when you do it often. Ways to save at the restaurant include the following:

- **Take advantage of discounts.** Use coupons from the paper if the restaurant is where you would normally dine.
- **Avoid major holidays.** Prices sometimes are escalated during those times, and the wait can be very frustrating. Just be mindful of others' feelings about this however! Don't ruin a special evening over a few dollars.
- **Change times.** Consider eating lunch instead of dinner. Prices usually are cheaper at noon than in the evening. Remember, higher demand will drive higher prices. Have dates with your spouse and meet for a quiet lunch once in a while. You will reap the benefits of socializing and conversation, without unneeded expenditures. Make it an adventure and enjoy!

- **Snack lightly before you go.** It will cut down on the temptation to over order and therefore overspend.
- **Ask for water with lemon.** This can really add up over time, and will not reduce your overall enjoyment of a meal out. Sodas are high profit items. For example, say you dine out four times per week. If sodas cost $1.49, this will translate into a savings of $309.92 per year, not including taxes! That alone pays my average water/sewer/trash bill for almost nine months.
- **Pass on alcohol.** Like coffee and deserts, these are high profit items, and you are paying dearly for it.
- **Consider eating an appetizer only.** Many appetizer plates are large enough for a meal.
- **Limit spending.** There is no need to buy the priciest item on the menu. Also, for items such as wine, there are several good ones on the lower-price scale—pricier isn't always better.
- **Split meals.** Most restaurants will split entrees for you in the kitchen. If not, ask for a second plate and do it yourself. Many times, there just simply is too much food to eat, and it invariably is wasted. Sharing with your spouse, date, or friend this way can cut your expenditure in half. We are sure that there will be at least one item that you will agree on that you both like to eat.
- **Drink coffee and have dessert at home.** These are high profit items for the restaurant owners. Plus, if you are watching calories, it is double savings.
- **Take home leftovers.** Ask for the doggy bag. It is perfectly acceptable. I've never been in a restaurant that

PLAYS TO EXECUTE
Entertainment

turned me down when asking for a to-go box. Obviously, this is for menu ordered and paid for items, not to load up a container from the all-you-can-eat buffet.

- **Give feedback on comment cards.** It is your chance to give constructive feedback to restaurant owners and managers. Sometimes you will be surprised to receive discount coupons in the mail.

Read Online

Local, regional, national and world news is at your fingertips on the web. If you just want to keep up to date, read online and avoid newsprint costs. Buy the paper only if you truly enjoy reading all of the "lesser news" over your routine cup of morning coffee.

Subscriptions

Stop buying newspaper and magazine subscriptions that you don't read. I limit myself to three magazines that I truly enjoy so I never feel that I have wasted money by not using something. Plus, I share one of those magazines with a friend, so we avoid the unnecessary expense, save space in the county landfill, and gain a good sense of sharing with someone.

Last-Minute Tickets

Call and ask if there are any last minute tickets available. The venue will gladly sell those at a discount rather than not have any revenue at all.

Off-Season Vacations

You work hard and need a vacation periodically. If you like to travel, consider off-season vacation destinations. Savings can be considerable if it can be worked out.

Visit the Local Library

This is a gold mine of information and entertainment. Aside from books, you can check out magazines, DVDs, CDs, artwork, posters, etc. You can also pick up items such as information about community events and preprinted income tax forms. You may be using a tax preparation software service, but if not, here is a great source.

General Finances

To have more dollars for something that you want or need, you must spend less on something else. That is a simple fact. Everyone has different methods that they choose to implement to save. Here are some ways to keep more of your dollars that use plain sense as related to your daily finances. Also, see the section on investing to make these savings work for you.

Don't Use Your ATM Card Out of Your Network

It is typical for both your bank and the out-of-network bank to charge you fees for withdrawals made at another bank. This is usually a very high fee percentage-wise for convenience. For example, a $2.50 charge by each bank for a $20 withdrawal adds up to 25%. Only do this if you are traveling and it does not make sense to carry a lot of cash. Even then, use your debit or credit card wisely to avoid paying with cash.

Bank Fees

Scrutinize all bank fees. Research methods to get those fees reduced, or change to another bank that offers a better checking account plan for instance.

Pay Bills Online

If possible, using this option will help eliminate late charges and saves you costs of envelopes and postage.

Use Discount Brokers

If you purchase stocks, use a discount broker. Do a search on the Internet to find one.

Check Bills

Scrutinize all bills for errors. Most bills are accurate, but take a moment to read over utility, mortgage, insurance, medical bills, etc. to determine if they make sense and are correct. Do not fear calling the provider and demanding correction if an error is discovered.

Get Cash Back at Merchants

Many merchants will allow you to get cash back when using your debit card to purchase merchandise at their business. It is typically fee free, and is convenient.

Don't Bounce Checks

Aside from the ethical aspect, banks today are looking for ways to keep their bottom line higher, and will charge you fees including overdraft protection. A few minutes spent tracking your check writing, deposits, automatic withdrawals and ATM usage, will let you avoid this costly fee.

Never Pay Credit Card Interest

OK, let's face facts. Credit cards, when used wisely, are both a wonderful and convenient tool. Used unwisely, they definitely will cause you financial hardship and loss in the form of high interest expenses. The average American has several credit cards and is paying the credit company dearly for the convenience. And to top it off, generally the balance is comprised of items that we consider to be on the "want" or "luxury" list, i.e. restaurant meals, new clothes, entertainment, etc. It is perfectly OK to have a credit card, as it can be used for convenient tracking of spending, and it is sometimes required such as for being able to rent a car. Also, if you always pay off the balance within the grace period, you get to use someone else's money interest free! Just be sure your credit card company allows this—read the fine print regarding the grace period and watch payment due dates. Note that the typical grace period, a time period that you have to pay off your balance before interest charges occur, has steadily decreased. It used to be 25 days or so, however, many credit card companies have reduced this time—some down to 14 days. Don't fall into the trap of not paying on time. The issuer does not mind if you have to pay late fees and/or interest. Plus … interest rates will tend to go up on your card if you pay late, again, lining the pockets of the issuer. Educate yourself regarding your specific card.

Use Credit Cards Wisely

Using a credit card has the likely potential of turning you into a different kind of shopper. Credit card users are less price sensitive and tend to spend more each time they pull out the plastic. In general, pull out cash instead of the card, and you will tend to spend much less. If you don't want to carry cash, use your debit card instead, and treat it with exactly the same mindset as cash. It all boils down to discipline. Using the debit card will force you to watch your bank balance closer. Remember, do not pay overdraft fees!

Use Savings or Other Sources

Use money in a savings or checking account to pay down credit card balances. You will save money by reducing your interest charges.

PLAYS TO EXECUTE
General Finances

Use Credit Cards with "Rewards"

Many credit card companies, including gasoline credit cards, will allow you to earn reward points that can be used for future purchases of airline tickets, car rentals, etc. Again, just be certain that you are using the credit card for purchases that you would normally make, are paying off your balance, and are not spending additional money by purchasing something that you would not do if you didn't have the points.

Credit Card Fees

Ask if you can get the annual fee waived and a lower interest rate. Credit card companies are after your business and will do everything they can to reasonably keep it. There are many companies vying for your business and generally will be willing to work with you. They are aware that you can move to a different carrier. Do your research and be prepared to switch companies if you can substantially reduce fees and interest rates.

Educate Yourself

Learn to use the Internet to your advantage. The information you can gather is unlimited. Use programs such as tax preparation software to do your own taxes. There are good ones that are very user friendly. Learn to fix minor problems around the house.

Negotiate All Interest Rates When Borrowing

If you must borrow money, shop for the best deals. A little time spent researching for the lowest rate will save you many dollars in finance charges, especially the longer the term of the note.

Get a Shorter Mortgage

If you have borrowed money for a home purchase some time ago, and interest rates have fallen, you may be able to refinance and save big on interest costs. There will be refinancing costs involved, but these are generally offset quickly by paying a lower interest rate. Check with your mortgage company; they will have advisors to explain the process. And, speaking of mortgages, make sure if you get a mortgage that you can pay it off or refinance without any penalties.

Membership Discounts

You may be able to get discounts on such things as car rentals, gasoline, restaurant meals, and hotel bills if you belong to a professional organization or are a senior citizen. Even "senior citizen" is defined by different organizations at different ages. Even though we don't want to admit we are getting older, take advantage of these discounts.

Save Overtime Pay

If you are paid overtime, set aside those extra earnings as savings. Even small amounts will add up over time and will help you gain more financial independence.

Never Be Late with Any Payments

A late charge is money wasted, plus a pattern of this can damage your credit rating.

Pay Yourself

Aside from your beliefs regarding tithing, charities, etc. make sure to pay yourself before making any "want" purchases. Get into the habit of setting an amount back in savings or investments regularly. Automatic payroll deductions, if allowed by your employer, are a great way to accomplish this. You will not be as tempted to spend money that is not as readily available.

PLAYS TO EXECUTE
General Finances

Save Your Next Raise

With the ever-increasing cost of living, this may be hard to do, but weren't you getting along in the last few months before the raise?

Sell It If Necessary

We all accumulate items that just plain become too expensive to maintain. If you no longer use the item, get rid of it. Examples are the second car rarely used, the overly large house since the kids are gone, etc. Downsizing will save you money.

Don't Get Shortchanged

Sadly, there are clerks or cashiers that are not properly educated in counting out change, or they are rushed, or flatly just don't care. Watch that your change is properly given back to you. You can easily lose several dollars in a bad transaction.

Buy and Use a Shredder

This tip has been told about time and time again lately in the news, on money saving websites, bank newsletters, etc. If you are a victim of ID theft, it is guaranteed to be both a time-consuming and expensive process. Yes, this may not initially SAVE you any money, since you have a cost outlay for the machine, but the cost is very minor in comparison to what you will lose if ID theft happens to you.

Never Get a Tax Refund

If you do, you have loaned the government YOUR money interest free. Discipline yourself to not plan to get a refund. You can adjust your withholdings by changing your Form W-4 at your place of employment. Check with the Human Resources or Payroll Department, they will be able to help you.

Typically, they will not give tax advice to you, but will give you new forms with instructions. Check with your tax advisor for further guidance if necessary. We can hear some of you saying that you use this as a "savings" plan and that you can't spend money if you don't have it. But we still maintain that it is a non-earning savings plan, and that you will be required to have great discipline to refrain from spending any tax refund when you receive it. Don't set yourself up to splurge with this money. It is better to have a plan to be able to put your money to good use, not the government.

Tax Refunds (If You Must)

Put those in a savings or investment account.

Drop Off Utility Bills at the Grocery Store

Many grocery or discount stores have a separate mail bin for local utility drop off payments. Make good use of those. At today's postage rates (and sure to increase), you can save a few dollars per month by using this convenience.

Food

One of nature's laws is that we all have to eat to survive. Not only is it necessary, but also it can be very pleasurable and also provides for good times in social settings and great family times. The real goal is to satisfy the hunger and to be able to eat good, healthy food without breaking the bank account. Food prices are no doubt heading higher, especially considering the increased costs of packaging and transportation due to the unprecedented rise in energy prices. There are numerous ideas that you can incorporate into your daily food routine to minimize your expenses.

PLAYS TO EXECUTE
Food

Bread

Watch for sales on bread. Stores will mark down fresh bread that is nearing the expiration date. You can save by watching for this "manager special" and buy several loaves and place them in your freezer. It will keep several weeks. Let them defrost fully at room temperature before using—it doesn't work well to defrost them in the microwave. Save heels from bread loaves, leftover crust from sandwiches, etc. and freeze them in an airtight bag. Use for salad croutons or for making stuffing at a later date. Buy bulk corn or flour tortillas. They will keep a long time in the refrigerator or you can divide and freeze.

Brown Bag It

If you have a job that allows you to brown bag your lunch, by all means do it. Consider that spending $2.00 a day for home-prepared meals, instead of $6.00 will help you save almost $1,000 per year if you do it every day. Just remember to still do some social lunch functions with co-workers or friends or you will become burned out by lunching in every day. Also, buy food containers that fit together and use the same size lids. This is just one thing that will help keep frustration low so you will be more likely to pack a lunch. I've brown-bagged for years, and the savings have been tremendous. I have been in the workforce for more than 25 years, and have brown-bagged during that time. I have not tracked what I have saved but just as an estimate, I have probably averaged brown bagging 4 days per week. By estimating savings (cost of eating out less cost of brown bag lunch for a savings of $3.00 per day), and doing some quick math, over a 25-year period, the cost savings has been $15,000.00. And don't forget, that is after tax money, and it is "simple" money, and does not consider any investment gains. Did that get your attention? This brings us back to another suggestion—Learn to Cook—and enjoy your leftovers as you fund an investment account.

Clearance Racks

Find the clearance racks at your favorite supermarket and check them out on each shopping trip. Usually, there is more than one. Check out the meat department, the bakery, the personal items section, etc. You can find bargains on meat, dairy, and produce items that are nearing the expiration date or on items that are being discontinued. If you have a freezer, you can save by purchasing meat items and storing them. The caveat: be sure that you have the room for items, and it is something that you would normally buy and will definitely use. Speaking of freezers, they can be very handy and a place to store your bargains if you have the space, such as in a garage or basement.

A used freezer can be a bargain as they generally last for years. I bought mine from a co-worker that wanted to get rid of it. I hesitated to buy it for a day, really because I was deciding where to put it and how to get it home, and the next day the price had dropped 50%! That was years ago, and it still purrs like a kitten.

Say No to the Specialty Coffee

There are several shops that charge just plain outrageous fees for a cup of coffee. Consider if it is really that important to spend several dollars per day for that pleasure. There are machines on the market that will allow you to make your own specialty drinks. If you must have specialty coffee, buy your own quality machine and brew up your own for considerable savings.

PLAYS TO EXECUTE
Food

Compost

All food preparation produces some amount of scraps, such as potato peelings. If you can, use these in a compost pile instead of the garbage disposal.

Learn to Cook

This is first and foremost, as eating out can take a huge bite out of anyone's food spending plan. This not only includes meals out at fancy restaurants, but those daily fast food purchases also. Any food out purchase can quickly add up. By learning to cook, you will also use far less pre-prepared foods. Remember, convenience almost always adds up to increased expenses. There is much to be said about a true home cooked meal that you provide either for yourself or your family. Start out with simple recipes from the Internet, or borrow some cookbooks. Trust us, most people who like to cook have an abundance of cookbooks that they will let you borrow or have a family member or friend give you advice. They will enjoy doing it and you will save money as a bonus.

Slow Cookers

Remember when the slow cooker was the rage? It was—and is—a wonderful invention. Drag it out of the back of the closet and put it to use. Recipes can be found on the Internet. Slow cookers are available in several sizes and are an inexpensive appliance purchase plus utility costs are very low. When in college (many years ago), my roommate and I cooked many meals in one of these. We made everything it seemed. And, it was handy as meals could be hot and ready when classes where over. We made chili, ham and beans, many types of stews and soups, roasts, chicken and noodles, vegetables, and the list goes on—I just can't remember all of it. Believe it or not, I still have the same cooker and it works like a charm to this day. Use it to marinade tougher (read cheaper) cuts of meat and they will turn out tender and delicious.

Coupons

Only use coupons when they make economic sense. Generally, generics or store brands will be cheaper. Use coupons only when it is for an item that you truly like and will use. It is not a bargain if you buy the item just because you have a coupon and then wind up wasting it. There are times when the use of a coupon will present a bargain opportunity, just be prudent with their use. Keep coupons for at least four weeks. For example, there is what is known as the "coupon rush" for brand items within a week of publishing. Merchandise often goes on sale after the coupon rush is over, and sometimes you can get the item free or almost free. Get coupons off of the Internet from retailers.

Shop at Discount Warehouses

These stores can be a bargain-hunter's delight. You will have to get used to the lower conveniences and their rules, but dollars are saved here. As with generic purchases, you can quickly learn what is an acceptable product. Get savvy on unit prices, as sometimes the unit sizing is different. Be prepared to spend cash or use your debit card, as some discount places will not take checks or credit cards.

Plant A Garden

If you have the space, plant a garden. Not only is it therapeutic, but can save many dollars. Plant what you like and is suitable for your growing area and seasons. Share your bounty with your neighbors; you might be surprised what you get in return from their gardens. Even apartments have balconies, and can be used for growing a few plants including herbs. Also, try shopping at your local farmer's market during spring, summer and fall. There will be a wide variety of seasonal, fresh produce for sale. This is a golden opportunity to share shopping time with a friend and support local growers. Ask them directly about the use of pesticides if that is a concern to you.

Buy Generic

Many generic foods are very high quality. You can certainly almost always save money by buying generic. Our suggestion is to try the generic, and if you don't like it or it doesn't meet or satisfy your needs, don't buy it again. Only buy one unit of the item that you want to test, and if it somehow isn't right, you haven't lost much. However, if it is OK, your satisfaction and potential future savings can really add up. We hear that many store brands are even preferred over the name brands. You decide. Saving just a little on all of your purchases will add up over time.

Make Fewer Trips to the Grocery Store

Staying out of the stores will help you cut down on impulse buys. Do some simple math; just $10 a week in impulse buys is $520 per year. Most shoppers go to the store at least three times per week. Not only does that provide an opportunity to overbuy, but it costs you not only in time but transportation as well.

Re-Purpose Leftovers

Many foods can be re-purposed to a future meal. For example, that leftover chicken broth from the slow cooker makes a great liquid for cooking rice to pair with stir-fry.

Cook Several Meals at Once

Cook more than you would for just one meal, and store the rest in the freezer—great plan for brown bagging, or when you need a meal in a hurry.

Substitute Other Proteins for Meat

Beans and other legumes are high in protein and can provide necessary proteins for your diet at a much-reduced rate over meats.

Check Unit Prices

Most stores will have tags that indicate the unit price, whether it is by the ounce, pound, or some other unit of measure. Just be certain that you will use the entire product. It makes no sense to buy a gallon of mustard if you only plan on using a couple of tablespoons. Generally, bulk buying will save you money, but not if you waste most of it.

Get Away From The Restaurant Routine

We all enjoy eating out, and it sure seems to be convenient and fun. Instead of eating out several times a week, why not go once and really make it a nicer treat. Consider buying restaurant coupon books from your local schools or scouts if they make economic sense and you will use enough coupons to cover the cost.

Time Your Restaurant Experience

Generally, you can save money by eating lunch out instead of dinner. You can get dinner quality for lunch prices. If it fits your schedule, meet your spouse, date, kids, etc. for lunch and save a bundle. Of course, eating at home is cheaper, but consider the social aspect.

PLAYS TO EXECUTE
Food

Buy Items That Are On Sale

Yes, generally you will like the particular food that is on sale. Just because you had on your list to buy apples, peaches may be on sale at a great bargain. Don't be afraid to alter your menu, as a little flexibility can go a long way in your saving plan. However, for example, if you've promised a child his or her favorite apples for doing a great job at chores, don't stray from the plan of bringing the apples home. Sale items usually can be found in the perimeter of the store. Always watch for sale tags but be aware of just how much something has been marked down, if at all. Aisle end cap items with a big sign aren't necessarily on sale, or a bargain. Expensive goods such as heavily processed, pre-packaged or already cooked are most often in center high traffic areas, right where you will see them easily. Be prepared to justify the costs when buying those items.

Buy Food in Season

Seasonal vegetables and fruits (fresh) are generally less expensive when there is a bountiful supply. If you desire out of season foods, consider buying frozen.

Shop with a List

Always be prepared when you go shopping. This will cut down on impulse buys. Know what ingredients you need for planned meals before you leave the house. Don't let children pressure you into buying what you don't need. You can customize your shopping to your favorite store so that you can get in and out quickly.

Carry Your Own Snacks

This includes to work, and to outings such as ball games. You can enjoy very healthy snacks at a much cheaper rate than buying from food vendors, convenience stores, or vending machines. If you have smaller children, buy fruit by the pound, not by piece. This will prevent wasted food because they may not eat all of a piece of fruit for example.

Specialty Items

Buy items off of the salad bar if you need only a small amount for a recipe or lunch. Items from the salad bar are sold by weight and you can save by just buying the amount that you need rather than a whole package.

Reduce Specialty Drinks

Sodas and other specialty drinks can be very expensive. Consider using mixes if those are to your liking. Also, tea is very cheap on a per glass basis and is considered a healthy beverage. And don't forget water; it is healthy and the cost is almost nil.

Bottled Water

Speaking of drinking water, what can we say about bottled water? It is currently much more expensive than gasoline per gallon, but it is being purchased by millions of gallons. No doubt, there are times it is convenient and necessary, but you can save a lot of dollars by using a water filter and recycling the bottles. And, the benefits to the environment go without further comment.

Cut Out Waste

Any wasted food is money down the drain. Plan ahead so that if you know you will have leftovers, it is a meal that suits being "left over" well. Teach your children that food is a blessing to have and that it also costs money. They will learn to follow your example. My father was very frugal and wasting anything was simply out of the question. Growing up on a farm, we had our own meat, dairy, and garden produce. We were always allowed to have plenty of food, but there was an unwritten rule. If you took food and put it on your plate, you had to eat it. Not necessarily at that meal or sitting, but at a later time. Second or third helpings were always allowed if you wanted. The lesson? We became very good at judging how much food to take, and to this day, I waste very little food. It not only saved money, but taught responsibility as well.

Giving

Giving money away is a highly personal activity that must be addressed by each individual. You should not only follow your capacity to give, but your heart in this sensitive matter. Everyone must determine what is right for him or her to do. There are countless places to contribute to and it includes not only money, but time, talents, concerns, and compassion. We will address a few of the ways to still give generously here with savings of your dollars in mind that use plain sense as related to your daily finances.

Give Gift Cards

In this manner, you can control the amount that you want to spend easily, and rest assured that the funds will be put to good use, provided you do a little research and determine what the recipient will truly like. It is proper to ask what stores that they like to shop at. If you are uncomfortable with asking, purchase a card to a grocery store or discount store as everyone can find something to their liking at those destinations. The more you know about the person, the easier it will be to purchase a certificate that they will appreciate.

Buy Greeting Cards at the Dollar Store

They are much cheaper there and many are very nice. You cannot argue with paying 50 cents vs. $2.99 if it is quality and fits the occasion.

Make Your Own Gifts

Most of us have some talent of some sort. Cooking or baking food items, selected crafts, or handyman services, etc. can be welcome gifts, especially for those not inclined to do those things or do them well. Gifts from the heart are welcomed. Pick up craft supplies at garage sales, or thrift stores—use your imagination!

Make Sure that You Get a Receipt for Tax Purposes

It is a fact in today's world that you need a receipt to deduct donations on your tax return to charities and churches. A cancelled check will no longer suffice. Give as you are led, but remember the tax authorities also.

Wrap Children's Gifts with the Sunday Comics

I started wrapping birthday and Christmas presents for my niece and nephews in comic strip newspaper. It creates another use for something that could possibly wind up in the landfill and saves money by not purchasing expensive wrapping paper. I continued this practice for several years when they were younger. One Christmas, I decided that they were getting "older" and I did not wrap their gifts in the comics. Boy, did I ever catch a lot of grief about it! I quickly found out that they liked the tradition, as they could always tell which gift was coming from their uncle. They are grown now, but I still sometimes wrap in the comics. Why not carry on fun traditions, and save money at the same time?

PLAYS TO EXECUTE
Giving

Give Plants as Gifts

Choose the ones that will last. Choose the ones that can be set outside and last for years. There are many types of plants that can be propagated and shared. Odds are if you like something, your friend, neighbor, or relative will like it too, since they will know that it came from someone special.

When it comes to saving money and deriving wealth from specific habits or practices, I cannot think of anything more enjoyable than that which comes from landscaping. I grew up as the only boy. For that reason I tended to be the one out in the yard—either mowing, pulling weeds, raking leaves or any other yard work project—whatever my mom, dad, or grandparents could come up with just to keep me busy.

I have since grown to derive great joy and accomplishment from landscaping. However, one challenge is knowing what to plant, when, where, and how. Quite honestly, all of this comes from sharing my experiences, talking about the projects I have done myself, or from what others might be working on. However, some of the most exotic plants can be quite expensive if one were to go down to the local nursery and pick out the exact size, shape, and variety of the shrub you might want.

I have, over time, approached this differently. As I travel or visit friends and family, I take notice and express true admiration of what others have done in their landscapes. I express this interest and ask if I might have a piece of the planting. To your surprise, you may find that many plants, trees, and shrubs can be propagated quite easily.

One of my favorites today is ornamental grasses. Tall, short, it does not matter to me. I look at the color and texture and can usually find a place in my own landscape to place it. Over the years that my plantings have grown, I have shared with others where I got them and from whom. I then divide them up and share them with others. Sometimes they have something else they share with me as well and the cycle continues.

It is quite cost effective, I must say, and I truly enjoy the relationships I have gained and cultivated over the years as well. I have received trees from people that have just popped up. They give them to me because of my interest, I suppose, and because they also know I will take good care of them and derive great joy and appreciation from them. Now when someone gives me something, I make sure and do my best to care for it. You never know when they might swing by and ask about it.

I have gotten maple trees, fruit trees, bushes and flowers. I was on the other side of town one day and stopped by an old friend's house. We were walking around his yard and talking about how "grown up" things were compared to the last visit. We stopped and talked about a specific plant. I expressed how much I liked it and how it had grown. To my surprise, he asked if I wanted it. Without a second thought, I said, "Sure." To his surprise, I took a shovel out of my truck and immediately uprooted the plant. We both laughed and savored the moment. I know this particular relationship will truly last a lifetime. I have that bush planted outside my back window and when I see it I appreciate my friend, friend for always. Thanks Joe. I have many stories like these and the list goes on and on.

My suggestion to all who are just starting out with a new home and landscaping is to be patient and cultivate your relationships as well as your landscape. The cost will be low and the grass will be green in your own backyard.

PLAYS TO EXECUTE
Giving

Re-Gifting

Ah, yes. The word drums up images of being frugal or cheap. This is a hot button topic among many people. However, we subscribe to the notion that it is OK. You just have to be careful and sensitive about it. We believe that if you have received a gift from someone and it is not useful in any way to you, there is no need to keep it. Just be careful not to give it back to the original giver. Of course, items considered antiques or heirlooms can more easily be re-gifted. You will occasionally receive an item that is inappropriate, too small or big, or is something that you already have. You can give it away to someone else, and therefore you are not letting the item go to waste or clutter up your home.

SOME RULES FOR RE-GIFTING:

- **Don't tell anyone it is a re-gift.** If it is in new condition (exception—an antique that you know the recipient would like), and it is appropriate, go ahead and give it with no guilt. No one needs to know where it came from.

- **Don't give something back to the person who gave it to you in the first place.**

- **Wrap it appropriately.** Don't put it in a box from the most expensive store in town. You are giving an appropriate gift—not showing off—and this will avoid embarrassment if the recipient tries to return it to a store. Also, be sure to use new wrapping paper and gift tags.

- **Don't give away junk.** This is not the time to clear out your attic. As with any gift, it must be considered appropriate to be appreciated.

- **Don't re-gift handmade, special or one-of-a-kind items.**

Health

Exercise

Numerous studies show that exercise will cut your ill-health risks down. You will pay fewer insurance co-pays and out of pocket expenses the healthier you remain. Join a gym, or exercise frequently outdoors. It is good for both physical and mental health.

Ways to Exercise

Find new ways to exercise, such as taking the stairs instead of the elevator, parking at the far side of the parking lot (when safe), walking the golf course instead of renting a cart, buying a push lawnmower, etc. Exercise for health, and healthier people obviously spend less money on health care.

Immediate Care Facilities

Learn where the nearest immediate care facilities are. Your health and safety should always come first, but using these types of facilities can reduce your health care costs.

Negotiate

Reports show that doctors and clinics will sometimes negotiate pricing (known as "reasonable and customary" charges) for medical services. This is especially true if you need to use services from a provider that is out of your network for health insurance. Your only potential loss is a few minutes of your time to ask for a reduced price.

OTCs

Educate yourself on over the counter (OTC) medications. You will save dollars by using those products instead of visiting the doctor for every malady. Seek advice from your licensed pharmacist—he or she will guide you to various acceptable products or will advise you to seek a physician's help if necessary.

Generic Prescriptions

Using generic prescriptions instead of name brands will significantly cut your costs. And if you use several prescriptions the savings are multiplied. Check with your doctor about using generics. Some discount retailers have implemented thirty day supplies of generics for a very minimal cost. The potential savings is tremendous—put a pencil to paper and figure what you will save.

Home

We've all heard, "Home is where the heart is," and it is true. Generally, home ownership is the largest expense for the average American. Expenditures can be very large depending upon your tastes and available funds. Regardless of your home's size, age or location, there are ways to make sure it is kept in good shape to avoid costly repairs and keep its value high.

No matter if you think of housekeeping and cleaning as a dreadful chore or not, it always seems to need to be done. Everyone enjoys a clean home. If you can discover ways to cut time and save money at the same time—great!

Aluminum Foil

To save on utilities, use aluminum foil to keep food warm. It saves energy over leaving the oven on.

Cleaners

Make your own household cleaners. Studies show that homemade cleaners will come close to matching commercial cleaners in most instances, plus they are cheaper and easier on the environment. Try out the old remedies. If they don't work for your application, you can always go to the stronger commercial version.

- **Soapy Ammonia**—Use this instead of an all-purpose cleaner for bathrooms and kitchens. Check out the label on household ammonia for specific directions. You can also place a small amount of mild liquid dish soap with water in a spray bottle. Use this to spray onto wooden or other hard-surface furniture. Wipe and then dry with a lint-free cloth. Test in a hidden place first and don't get furniture overly wet.

- **Baking Soda**—Cheap for freshening or cleaning the refrigerator.

- **Man-Made Chamois**—The natural chamois commonly used for drying automobiles tends to dry out and become scratchy. The synthetic chamois is very soft, works very well, and is easily washed in the washer, and can be (should be) placed back into its container ready for the next use. Works well on many hard surfaces.

- **Cloths**—Get some of the new-fangled microfiber cleaning cloths. They grab dirt with a passion, don't scratch, and are easily washed. They come in festive colors which gives a boost to your sense of accomplishment.

- **Freshen**—Freshen the house with simmering cinnamon. Healthier and cheaper than aerosol fresheners.

- **Glass Cleaner**—Use ¼ cup of soapy ammonia and ½ pint of rubbing alcohol per half gallon of water. Use in a spray bottle. Clean glass for no streaks by wiping dry with old pieces of newspaper.

PLAYS TO EXECUTE
Home

- **Sinks**—Try cleaning by soaking a layer of paper towels in hydrogen peroxide. Rinse after 15 minutes or maybe a little longer.
- **Toilets**—For stubborn stains, try placing a couple of denture-cleaning tablets in the toilet at night and flush away in the morning. Or, better yet, try cheap white vinegar. Use a couple of cups or so, let sit overnight and flush away in the morning.
- **T-Shirts**—Use old cotton T-shirts for wiping and scrubbing. They are very soft and can be easily washed.
- **Vinegar**—Dilute with 50% water and use to spray countertops. Use to clean glass. Use in laundry for a natural bleach. The acidity will kill germs. Make sure to always read labels, never mix chlorine bleach with any product. Remember, safety first, accidents are never money savers.

Decorating

When remodeling, consider repainting existing light fixtures. You will have a new look, and it is considerably cheaper. The major plus is, you know that everything already fits! Mirrors add reflective light and therefore you need less lighting. Buy them at flea markets, thrift stores, or antique shops and refinish them for the look that fits your décor.

Avoid Dirt

Tracking in mud and dirt wears your carpet and floors faster. And who wants the extra expense and waste of time cleaning the mess? Houses and furnishings are expensive—take care of what you own.

Stop Drafts

Check in spring or fall and update any areas that need caulking or weather stripping. Even small drafts are large energy wasters.

Fad

Think twice when tempted to paint with faddish colors, especially the exterior. The need to update happens more frequently (read costly) and can significantly lower your home's value if you need to sell and do not have the time or funds to update quickly.

Fans

Use ceiling or other fans to keep air flowing. You will be able to raise the temperature in summer by several degrees and still feel comfortable. Reverse ceiling fans in winter and run on low speed to circulate warmer air that naturally rises to ceiling levels.

Guttering

Keep guttering in good shape and cleaned out. Backed up guttering will eventually cause a need for expensive repairs such as wood rot, roof leaks or water drainage problems.

Humidifier

Use a humidifier in the winter to keep humidity at an acceptable level. Drier air tends to feel colder, and you will undoubtedly raise the thermostat for comfort and therefore waste unneeded heating costs. Always check with your physician if you have health concerns or requirements regarding humidity levels.

Insulation

Update any insulation needs, especially in the ceiling. Make sure the insulation has an "R" factor rating of at least 19 or more.

Consider insulation under floors above crawl space if proper ventilation will allow.

Paint and Caulking

Use good-quality paint and other supplies such as caulking when painting or repairing. Many are guaranteed for a certain number of years. Painting and other general repairs are time consuming and expensive, so avoid unnecessary costs by not only doing them when needed but completing the task with an acceptable job. The quality of the paint you use is very important.

Paper & Plastic Products

Be mindful of all of the paper and plastic products that you consume. Examples are plastic bags and wraps, paper cups, towels, bags, tissues, toilet paper, etc. They are convenient, but be mindful of the price. Buy the lowest quality that fits your needs and buy wisely in bulk. And conserve. Just because you got a great deal on 90 rolls of paper towels doesn't mean you should use them wastefully.

Rent Out

Renting out a spare room can save you countless dollars not to mention the rent income. Utilities can be shared along with maintenance. We won't go into all of the plusses and minuses of this type of arrangement here, as this is more of a personal nature.

Rent vs. Buy

We have gone around and around when it comes to either renting or owning a home. We have always ended up with the same result, however, and that is to be an owner. Quite frankly, as we made our considerations ultimately it came back to one word. That word is "responsibility." You might ask yourself what "responsibility" has to do with owning a home, and I would have to exclaim,

"Everything." Now we considered the fact that when you own a home you are responsible for the interest, taxes, maintenance, etc. Whereas, when you are renting, you are responsible for ... oh yeah, the rent. However, think about it. The rent includes interest, taxes, insurance, maintenance, etc. for the owner. What you do not get when you rent is the opportunity for appreciation of the specific real estate.

Air Vents

Keep clean for proper air flow which contributes to the efficiency of your heating and air conditioning system which saves money on energy.

Insurance

Insurance has been called the "necessary evil" expense. Everyone buys it and then hopes that they will never need it. There's not much you can do about the need for selected insurance. For example, you are required by law to have liability insurance coverage on your automobile and also full coverage on auto and home if you have a lien or mortgage. There are ways to get better deals. Competition seems to have kept premiums reasonably low. Revisit all of your insurance needs and coverage as it is easy to miss money-saving opportunities.

Auto Insurance

ASSESS COVERAGE ON OLDER VEHICLES

You can drop coverage for collision and comprehensive (provided you don't have a lien or are subject to state or local law requirements). If your vehicle is worth less than eight to ten times what it would cost to insure annually, consider deleting your collision and comprehensive coverage. No one knows when and accident or disaster will occur, but this just makes economic sense.

CHANGE THE DEDUCTIBLE

You need insurance to protect you from a major loss, not a broken window or a small dent in the fender. Raising your deductible from $250 to $1,000 could save you a large percentage on your premiums. You are also allowed to change your deductible, for example, during the spring time when you are more at risk for hail damages. Just be aware that you might have to stop by your agent's office to prove that you don't already have damage. They have the right to protect themselves from fraudulent claims.

DISCOUNTS

Premiums can be reduced for having things like anti-lock braking systems, air bag restraints, having been accident-free for a specified length of time, having a good driving record, and having taken defensive driving courses. Check with your agent to see what discounts are offered. They may not advise you unless you ask. Remember, they want your business and that they are working for you.

GET QUOTES

Check with other agents. Have them give you quotes for your coverage requirements. Usually, there is no charge and taking a small amount of time could potentially lead to big savings. Consider checking with family and friends to see where they have insurance.

COMBINING AUTO AND HOMEOWNER POLICIES

Let your agent know you are interested in getting a quote for combined coverage and you are shopping for the best rates available with other companies, often bundling like this provides a discount.

Child Life Insurance

Although this is a personal matter, it is not generally recommended that you purchase life insurance on children, unless they contribute to the family income. This concept may sound harsh, but fortunately, chances are that you will not need this coverage. You might consider having enough coverage to pay for burial expenses, if you have limited funds and these expenses would cause a large burden for you. Or, you could start a savings account, and put the money that you would spend on premiums into that each month.

Check Out Any Insurer with Your State Insurance Commissioner Web Site

They will give you a ratio of how many complaints are received compared to number of policies that they have written. Also, check with the Better Business Bureau.

Investing

Enroll in a 401(k) Or Other Similar Plan

Use the plans that your employer provides to your advantage to save. By signing up for a 401(k) plan for example, you will be deferring taxes on your contributions with a traditional 401(k) and savings is automatic. (A Roth 401(k) will not have the tax deferral, but withdrawals can be tax-free when you retire.) You should not take a loan against these funds, as you will lose out on the tax-deferred earnings compounding potential. Most employers will provide for matching of a certain percentage of your contributions. It is wise to save at least an amount to get the full employer match allowed. By not doing this, you are effectively turning down a raise.

We realize that it may be wise in certain situations to not contribute to the available savings plan. An example is if you have a large credit card debt and are paying a high interest rate, you need to pay off that balance first. Also, if you are just starting out in your job or career, you may need to delay savings to build your emergency fund or to get things you truly need to live. However, most employees can quickly put themselves in a situation to save. We know of people that will turn down the opportunity to invest and therefore miss out on the company match.

Let's assume for a moment that you earn $10.00 per hour, which translates into $20,800 per year if you only work standard hours. All plans vary, but let's assume that you can put up to 6% of your earnings into the plan with a 50% match. That will figure out to $624 per year that your employer will throw into the pot. This is calculated by taking the earnings of $20,800 times 6% and then multiply by 50%. Who does not want to earn another $624 per year? If you earn more, or are allowed to contribute more, the savings obviously will be higher. And don't forget compounding over a period of years.

If you turn down that matching opportunity, you will NEVER be able to get it back for the period that you did not participate. Opportunity knocks loudly sometimes. A former boss once said that not cutting expenses in the business when it was feasible and wise was exactly like burning up money. Related to that would be not taking the company match. To put it into perspective, money not taken in this manner is just the same as sitting at your kitchen table with a candle in front of you and slowly burning up some dollar bills. We'll bet that you never thought of it that way before, and we'll also bet that you haven't ever sat at the table watching greenbacks go up in smoke either.

Consider Index Mutual Funds

No one can know all of the ups and downs of the stock market, and when they will occur. Investing in a quality index mutual fund can be a way to invest wisely. Generally speaking, when you are determining what investment(s) to make, one of the biggest considerations people have to make is what the rate of return is expected to be. Part of the question is, "Based on what?" Or, "Compared to what?" If you are comparing the rate of return to having it accumulating in a fruit jar or under your mattress, any rate of return is better than that. Maybe not safer or more liquid, but is a better rate of return. If you are comparing it to inflation, however, you must immediately realize that a 3% to 5% rate of return is normally needed just to protect the buying power of your funds.

A common comparison to make is one of to "the market." Some may be saying, define "the market." We all have heard of the stock market and may even get a glimpse of it every night on the evening news. When we are asked or are concerned as how "the market" did today, we have to ask ourselves, "Compared to what?" The usual answer might be compared to yesterday, or compared to last year, or how "it" is doing this year. Up or down? When we get the answer it is usually like this: "it" was up 100 points, etc. That answer more than likely is how the "Dow" performed.

The "Dow" just for clarification refers to the Dow Jones Industrial average—originating in 1896 when Charles Dow compared the top 12 US companies and their performance to other companies. Since then it has grown to include the top 30 US companies which change over time based on how reflective each is of the market or their particular industry.

It is upon this which we base our suggestions to consider index funds as a potential investment. Many investment companies have created such investments which are based on trending how the market trends. The "Dow" is based on 30 US companies. The S&P 500 is just that, a compilation of a group of top performing 500 companies. There are foreign funds, industry funds, funds that include 2,000 companies and even 5,000 companies. The point here is to include this as part of your consideration when determining where you should invest to yield higher returns and greater diversification.

Invest in an IRA

Investing in a traditional or a Roth IRA can considerably cut your taxes, either up front or when you withdraw funds, depending on the type that you choose. Check with your tax advisor for specifics on each of these types of plans. IRAs can provide an avenue for lower taxes, and effectively makes you think twice on withdrawing retirement funds, due to taxes and potential penalties.

Lawn

A beautiful lawn to go along with a beautiful house—a traditional definition of the American Dream. Many people like to see a great landscape and be able to watch things grow, and spend time outdoors enjoying it. Landscaping costs and maintenance can take a considerable amount of money, basically unlimited depending on the size of your lawn and the quality desired. Although you should maintain a reasonable landscape to fit your neighborhood and help keep your property values up, most expenses are personal preference. Keep in mind the following:

Read Directions

Read and follow all applications for various fertilizers, herbicides and insecticides. Over-applying does not translate into better results and only contributes to both damage to the environment and your checkbook. In some cases, it is illegal to over-apply. Why break the bank to break the rules?

Wash the Fertilizer Spreader

If you use a fertilizer/seed spreader, wash it after each use and let dry thoroughly before storing away. Fertilizers are caustic and will rust delicate parts and make it unusable. A former co-worker scoffed at this idea until I asked her how many spreaders they had purchased in the last twenty years. Her response was "several." I have purchased only one.

Grill

Cover the grill when not in use or better yet, store in a storage shed or garage. It will last much longer. Just be careful not to place a hot grill inside.

Maintain the Lawnmower

Just as you need to maintain your automobile, you need to maintain the mower and other yard equipment. Keep the blades sharp. This not only puts less strain on the engine but is more healthy for the grass. Healthy lawn equals more enjoyment and less expense. Change the oil and filters regularly, especially if you mow frequently in dry, dusty conditions. They will last many more seasons with a touch of proper maintenance. Also, pick up debris before mowing, hitting a large object not only puts you in danger, but can ruin engine shafts.

PLAYS TO EXECUTE
Lawn

Buy Quality

Buy quality seeds and plants. Healthy plantings will provide a better looking landscape and save replacement costs and frustrations. Your local nursery is an excellent source on plants that will fit your growing area, types of soils, your preferences, water needs, etc. Many plants are transplantable. Get with a friend or neighbor and share seeds, plants or "starts." For plants that need thinned out, this is an excellent way to share.

Tanks

Have two separate tanks of fuel for the grille. As they are easily changed, this will save you money as you will not be tempted to return a partially used canister just to make sure you don't run out of fuel on an important party night.

Tools

Keep lawn tools clean and in proper working order. As with all tool purchases, buy the quality you need that will fit the job at hand.

Watering

Don't over water the lawn. Usually, one inch per week is sufficient to keep the lawn alive.

Office

Everyone seems to be drowning in more and more paperwork these days. No doubt your home office is getting more cluttered and complicated. We have more bills and other requirements to take care of every day it seems. Insurance, utilities, mortgage, car, education, investments, all of these items require paperwork. To take care of, dare we say, all of this mess, there are things that you can do to cut back on the expenses it takes to maintain all of it. Ways to save money include the following:

Printer Ink

The computer is apparently here to stay, and supplies to make good use of it are in ever increasing demand and expense. Our society definitely has not gone paperless; it is worse than ever. Don't use color ink unless you are sure that what you want to print looks right on the screen. Use the greyscale printing option if you must print to review your documents.

Scratch Paper

Use scratch paper for making notes, writing drafts, making mathematical calculations, etc. There is no need to waste new paper for these things. Keep a handy stash of paper to use in these instances.

Backup

Stagger the use of backup media such as rewritable CDs for computer backup. Keep these in a safe place in case there is a need to retrieve lost files.

Check Printing

Save on check printing fees by getting free checks and supplies on selected bank checking accounts. Or use discount check printers. There are usually ads that have their services listed in the coupon sections of the Sunday paper. You can save check costs by paying online, but there still are instances where you need to have a paper check.

Seasonal Buys

Back-to-school time is an excellent time to purchase office supplies. Many stores in our area will offer spiral notebooks

PLAYS TO EXECUTE
Office

for 10 cents each in August or early September. That is just unbeatable. Of course, it is a marketing ploy to get you into the store to buy other things, but you can win if you watch your other spending.

Lower Quality

Use the lowest quality/priced paper that fits the application. Cheaper paper for your daily needs will usually suffice. Save your money for other needs such as a quality paper for those resumes that you are sending out.

E-mail

Learn to use e-mail and sharing of files. This saves on paper, ink, and postage, not to mention the convenience.

Personal

Items and services of a personal nature are, to say the very least, personal. In this category are items that cannot be placed in other sections such as clothing, household, medical, health, etc.

Exercise Programs

Exercising is healthy and in general will cut medical costs over a long period of time. Buy what clothing and equipment you need. Ask for discounts at the gym, especially at New Year's. Some will give healthy discounts if you pay for a year in advance. Discipline yourself to use the facilities regularly. However, be careful here. You will only have made a good deal if you KNOW you will use a full year membership and you actually follow through with it.

Hygiene

Good personal hygiene is essential. Not only will you feel better, but you will save money on medical costs. Face it, soap and water are cheap. Use them frequently to cut down on illnesses such as colds.

Lens Cloths

Use a quality lens cloth to clean eyeglasses. This will cut down scratches and needless replacement of lenses.

Professional

Consider getting haircuts, massages, manicures, etc. at training schools. These services are heavily supervised and can be had at a great discount. Plus, there is no tipping allowed either.

Razor Blades

Re-use razor blades several times. Replace only when satisfactory results are unattainable.

Sample Size

Avoid buying sample sizes for travel such as shampoos, lotions, tissues, etc. Refill with bulk purchases into the smaller containers that you probably already have.

Trimming

Buy a set of quality, adjustable hair clippers that come with attachments. These will come in very handy for doing "touch ups," especially for men and boys. You can quickly learn how to trim necks and sideburns, etc. to get a fresh look without spending big dollars at the barbershop. You can easily stretch periods between cuts by a couple of weeks and over time, save a bundle. Instructions will come with the trimmers.

Tax Planning

Death and taxes—they say we can't avoid either one. But with a good strategy you can cut your bills for taxes. There are many

PLAYS TO EXECUTE
Personal & Tax Planning

facets and strategies which are useful in planning for, paying, and even reducing your tax burden. However, just the burden of figuring out what to do can become very complicated. Needless to say, we feel that the government in many ways has complicated the tax system way beyond what it should be. We live in a very complicated, man-made-set-of-rules world, and it doesn't seem to be getting any better regardless of what any political office holder or candidate might be telling you.

This book is not a technical guideline with explanations of laws, where the best investments might be, or exactly what you should spend your money on, etc. It is to get you into the game, and enable you to wisely plan for your future. Unless you are an expert, or willing to do a lot of research and studying, we recommend that you consult with qualified professionals regarding taxes, including but not limited to personal income tax, tax deferred investments such as a 401(k), gift taxes, and inheritance or estate taxes.

Not everyone will have a need to strategize for every tax, as some might not pertain to your situation. However, please keep in mind that as your financial situation changes, or as you near retirement, or retire, you will need to plan for everything that might affect you.

The following is a list of things that you should consider while in the process of tax planning. Again, this is not a complete list but just a place to start.

1) **Planning for payments of taxes, for example through withholdings from your paycheck by your employer or payments of estimated income taxes.**

2) **Use of tax deferred instruments such as a 401(k) or deferred compensation plan.**

3) **Taking advantage of the capital gains tax.**

4) **Contributions to (or withdrawals from) pensions and annuities.**

5) **Use of Health Savings Accounts.**

6) **Conversions of IRA accounts to Roth IRA accounts.**

7) **Giving of gifts to reduce estate taxes.**

8) **Saving in taxable vs. non-taxable investments.**

9) **Maximizing deductions.**

10) **Taking advantage of certain tax credits.**

There are several tax programs that you can purchase that can help you perform tax-saving strategies and help you prepare your returns. Most people will find these software programs to be very beneficial unless you have very complicated issues regarding your tax obligations.

Travel

Travel Off-Season

By traveling during off-seasons, not only will you avoid bigger crowds, but you will see considerable discounting for hotels, passes, entertainment, etc.

Vacation Close to Home

The new buzz word seems to be "staycation." With ever-increasing airline and gasoline costs, staying close to home makes all the more sense. Even a mini-vacation can be fun. Occasionally, I will get together with friends for a day or two and we will pretend that we are tourists in our own city or immediate area. We have discovered that there are many places to see that we hadn't considered before. No travel costs to a far away destination, no travel time, no travel security frustrations, no lodging expenditures. Wow!

PLAYS TO EXECUTE
Travel

Utilities

Utility expenses continue to march upward just like food and gasoline. Driven by higher costs of natural resources, labor, insurance, etc., the utility companies are forced to raise prices to survive just like any other business. Although many are government regulated, the regulators are allowing increased prices. This obviously means more dollars being pulled out of your wallet. As with other expenses, there certainly are ways to minimize that pull. There are numerous ways to cut back on utility costs, and of course, every dollar saved can be used as needed somewhere else or better yet, invested. Consider and implement wherever possible the following ways to slash your overall utility bills.

Buy Appliances with the Energy Star Rating

The Energy Star rated appliances and other electronic devices are recognized by the Environmental Protection Agency as meeting their standards for efficiency. Buying these can potentially save you hundreds of dollars per year on electricity costs as compared to ones that do not have this rating.

Assess Your Cable TV Bill

Seriously now, how many of those 120 plus channels do you really need or really watch? I do not have cable TV, and I still seem to have plenty to watch if I want. Of course, when visiting friends or staying in a motel room, it's fun to channel surf, but invariably, more time is spent surfing than actually watching and enjoying a show. You might say that it happens because of the novelty, but I believe more often than not it also happens in your home on a regular basis. Cut what you don't need.

TV/Cable/Internet Bundles

The telephone companies no longer just provide simple telephone services. Most will have packages that can save you money by bundling services that you need. Ask what they can do for you.

The Luxury Cell Phone

A cell phone can definitely be a useful tool, especially when needed for true emergencies. No doubt, they can even cut other costs such as communicating who is to pick up the kids from somewhere, so that you both don't waste an expensive car trip to the same place. However, most plans come with many expensive, add-on features which you never use. We advocate having a cell phone with only the basic features that you actually use. Also, cut down your time on the phone. Believe us, just a short time ago, the average American was not on the phone talking about unimportant "this and that" to everyone and their brother. Discipline every aspect of phone usage. For example, get a calling plan that has free minutes and free long distance and make the best use of those times. Call your mother, your best friend, whomever, just do it when it is free! Eliminate or cut way down on the text messaging. I will say that you can cut out a huge percentage of those and never miss it.

Eliminate the Landline Phone

Assess your need for what is becoming an "old fashioned" phone. Only you can decide if having only a cell phone will be appropriate for your needs. If you don't have the need for a landline, eliminating this can potentially save you hundreds of dollars a year.

Shop Phone Companies

Not all phone companies are created equal. You have a multitude of choices in today's competitive world for communication services.

Look in the business listing section of the phone book and call those providers and ask what they can do for you. Be prepared to answer questions as to what services you are in the market for. Do you need Internet services and what type or speed? Do you need a low long distance rate? Are you willing to pay a flat monthly fee for lower long distance? Do you make international calls?

Unplug Computers

Many appliances and electronics are in what is known as standby mode, so that they will start quickly when needed. However, when you add up all of those devices in your home the energy consumption can really add up. Consider use of a power strip that has one switch that will turn everything off at once when not needed. An example is the computer, modem, printer, etc.

Stop Drips

Dripping water is money literally down the drain, not to mention the annoying sound of it, especially the toilet refilling every little bit. And, dripping HOT water is a double-edged sword of expense.

Use a Faucet Aerator

Use of the little device on faucets known as an aerator cuts the flow of water and provides better cleaning and rinsing power. Plus, they cut down on water heating costs as you will use less hot water. They can be purchased at the hardware or discount store and easily installed on most standard faucets.

Install a Whole House Fan

One way to conserve on air conditioning bills is to use a whole house fan. These are usually placed in a hallway and open up into the attic. By opening selected windows, you direct the flow of air coming into the house and out through the attic whereever you need cool air. This works especially well in the spring and fall, when temperatures are warm but not overly hot. You will have electricity costs to operate the fan, but it is not nearly as much as the AC. I have used one in my home for many years and have found it to be a very efficient way to keep the house comfortable in selected seasons.

Service the HVAC System

A properly serviced and running heating and cooling system will lower your energy consumption. Have the burners and the fan blades cleaned at least once a year. The coolant pressure and levels should be checked. And that filter, change it when it is dirty. Also, consider a filter that is reusable. There are different brands on the market that will do a great job of filtering and can easily be washed frequently. Be sure that you buy the proper size for your HVAC unit. Keep your central air conditioning unit clean to keep it at peak performance. Ductwork should be fully sealed to avoid loss of cooled air and make sure that all ductwork in non-cooled spaces is properly insulated. Also, check that all weather stripping around doors, windows and other openings is airtight. The condenser unit of the AC system that is outside of your home must be kept clear of leaves, dirt, lint, and other debris. Clogged condensers force the unit to run longer and less efficiently. Check the drainpipe once in a while for blockages.

Install a Set Back Thermostat

There are many types of HVAC thermostats on the market that will tremendously save utility costs. These work by lowering the temperature at selected times in the winter and raising the temperature at selected times during the summer. For example,

PLAYS TO EXECUTE
Utilities

you can have the temperature lowered at bedtime automatically and be raised before you arise in the morning.

Use an Electric Blanket

This, in combination with a set back thermostat, will keep you comfortable and save energy costs.

Assess Lawn Watering

We all enjoy nature to some extent, and a green lawn is pleasing to the eye. But with today's increasing water shortages and escalating bills, it may be less important now and in the future to sacrifice a little green in the lawn for some more green in the pocket. Enjoy your lawn and outdoors, but the need for a totally lush, large area needs to be given thought.

Use Compact Fluorescent Lighting

CFL bulbs use approximately one fourth of the energy than conventional incandescent bulbs. Yes, they cost more, but the savings over the life of the bulb more than offset the costs. There are several different types of the CFL bulbs; buy the ones that fit your needs. For example, use one made for reading in the lamp next to your favorite chair where you read, and use a different type in the kitchen or bedroom. Recommended uses are labeled on the bulb packaging.

Turn-Off Lights

When leaving the room for more than a few minutes at a time, turn off the lights. Why pay to light a room when no one is there? This is an easy habit to get into, and every less kilowatt used is money saved.

Use Light Timers

If you are going to be away from home, using light timers will save electricity as opposed to leaving lights on. Plus, there is an advantage of the appearance that someone is home, and cuts your burglary and vandalism risks. They can be set to turn lights on at several intervals per evening or night.

Use a Microwave or Toaster Oven

By using these efficient appliances you will be using less energy than by heating or reheating with a conventional oven or stove.

Power Supplies

Power supplies are those little black boxes that convert AC wall current into low-voltage DC and work as chargers or power for computer monitors, printers, battery chargers, and all sorts of appliances. They draw current when they are plugged in whether you are using their output current or not (they are often warm when plugged in even if they are not in use). Either unplug these when not in use, or like with one that powers a computer monitor, plug it into a power strip with your computer so you can turn it off without having to unplug it.

Close-Off Unused Rooms

Why pay to heat or cool space that you are not going to be in? You can close off a room or two and save big. One word of caution though: Just be sure that your heating/cooling system will operate efficiently by doing this, e.g. airflow issues. I recommend having an energy audit done. The experts can tell you if this is wise.

Raise the Temperature in the Refrigerator

The refrigerator compartment can safely be set at forty degrees. This is especially true if you do not open the door frequently. If you do open frequently, consider setting a couple of degrees cooler. Newer refrigerators are much more energy efficient, but use a proper setting to save money. The freezer section temperature can be set independently of the refrigerator section. Buy an inexpensive thermometer (or borrow one temporarily from a friend or neighbor) and adjust as necessary. Check the seals by closing a dollar bill in the door. If you can pull it out easily, replace the seals.

Low-Flow Showerheads

Install a low flow showerhead, and you will save on the water bill plus the water heating costs. Enjoy your shower, it is relaxing, just don't stay in there all morning!

Share Trash Service

Consider sharing trash service with a neighbor if you infrequently fill the dumpster.

Lower the Temperature of the Water Heater

Have you ever been in a home (including yours) that when you wash your hands, the water temperature is unbearably hot unless you mix with a big twist of the "cold" faucet? That translates into wasted money. Gradually lower the thermostat on the water heater over a period of several days, so that you can judge how much is tolerable and still have a reasonable temperature for showers, etc.

Insulate the Water Heater

There are several brands and insulating properties of blankets made for reducing heat loss from the water heater. Measure your tank circumference and height and have someone at a discount hardware store help you with selection.

Run a Full Dishwasher

Needless to say maybe, but running this appliance not at full capacity will increase your energy costs and wear and tear on the machine. Of course, if you do not use many dishes per day, you won't want to leave them there for a week before cleaning! Common sense says, "Avoid a terrible smell."

Run a Full Clothes Washer

Ditto from the hints on running a full dishwasher.

Use Less Laundry Detergent

Remember, the soap company is in the business of selling their product and making a profit. Studies show that using up to one-half less of the recommended amount of laundry detergent will get your clothes just as clean. Try it. The only thing that you will potentially lose is a load of not quite as clean clothes. Try a different brand, and you will find one that gets the results that you are looking for.

Wash Clothes in Cold Water

Again, try it on a few selected loads. You will find that clothes come out clean and will last longer. Hot water breaks down fabrics.

Use the Moisture Sensor Feature

Many clothes dryers are equipped with a setting that shuts the machine off when clothes are dry, as opposed to a set time. Since the dryer is a large energy user, use of this feature will help save costs. And, an added benefit is that your clothes will look better and last longer due to less wear and tear during tumbling. That dryer lint that you clean out frequently comes from somewhere, and it is from broken down fabrics on costly clothing.

Clean Dryer Lint Screen

Each time you use your dryer, check the lint screen and clean as necessary. Excess lint buildup prevents proper airflow and therefore your dryer will not be able to vent moisture properly, therefore using more energy. Also, periodically clean the ducts to better improve airflow and lessen the risk of fire danger.

PLAYS TO EXECUTE
Utilities

CHAPTER EIGHT
The Winning Triumph

To win the game, how will you determine the triumphant outcome of your efforts and how to use them? Will you pursue only material things—in essence chasing the usual worldly definition of the dream? Or will you desire a fuller, broader sense of accomplishment and joy? Which will it be for you in this game of becoming wealthy? The joy of important things (**FAITH, FITNESS, FAMILY, FRIENDS**) is crucial. Yes, it does take a job, work, and a medium of exchange as a part of the whole equation, but those are only a part of what it takes to win. Use those as tools to accomplish the win.

Set goals and strive for that triumphant win. Along the way you will have lots of moments of happiness. Let them "happen" for you. Enjoy as you go. Do not make "I must be happy" your mantra. Let happiness happen. You cannot make it happen. It is not something you can catch and put into a jar. And no one has it at all times.

There are lots of "joyous moments," however. For example, we talk about the stock market going up and down, the ebb and flow of the economy, and people's moods about investing. Remember that stock trades can *only* happen when there is a willing seller *and* a willing buyer. It is two sided. To get a joyous moment you must buy at some lower points (be happy when the market is down for that) and then sell at a higher point. The joyous moment happens when the market goes up.

True wealth can happen at any time during life. It happens sometimes when you least expect it. There are moments of joy that are what would or could be considered small things or large things and everything in between. Examples are everything from a phone call from a friend to the joy of the birth of a child. The "larger ones" such as college graduation, getting married, having children, accomplishing a long-term goal, mastering a craft, etc. are all benchmarks in your life. Celebrate them, and fill life in around all of those benchmarks with lots of the smaller happenings. In other words, stop and smell the roses.

When you win at your game, you might just have chills running through your body. It is a moment in time with a real feeling of a sense of accomplishment. Finally being the champion, whether it is a "small win" or a "big win," it is a great feeling to finally finish your project. Believe what you have just accomplished and savor the victory. Then move on to the next one.

You will need teammates to make the impossible possible sometimes. Those are your network of family, friends, advisors, neighbors, agents, bankers; the list goes on. Let them help you along the way, and help them in return. They will be pleased that you have won your game. And along that way, you can help them win theirs also.

Expect your championship. If you have laid basic groundwork by following the **FUNDAMENTALS** that we have discussed, you are bound to succeed. Your honest answer to yourself and others will be that you are poised for triumph. You must, at some point during your game, begin to believe. Take in the experience. Every part of your game will have its challenges. Learn from every mistake. Do not worry that your game will come to an end before victory. Get pumped up no matter what quarter you are in and keep moving forward. Keep listening to your cheerleaders; they really will keep you focused. Let your fans push you to the championship.

Let your triumph be what you want it to be and thank your Creator for answering your prayers in a positive way. It will be something that you will always remember.

That brings us to leaving a legacy. And that doesn't just mean to your children, as some do not have those. You can leave ideas, memories, funds, etc. to relatives, friends, or co-workers—what you want them to have and also remember about you.

The book of Ecclesiastes in the Bible teaches that there is an appointed time for everything. Although there may be many interpretations of this scripture, we believe it contains wisdom for everyone by relating how to handle many situations in life. Life contains a lot of difficulties, unexpected turns, but also a lot of joys. Hope in God will help you keep your life from slipping into cycles of despair. Chapter 3, verses 1 through 14 from the New International Version says:

> **There is a time for everything, and a season for every activity under heaven:**
>
> **A time to be born and a time to die,**
>
> **A time to plant and a time to uproot,**
>
> **A time to kill and a time to heal,**
>
> **A time to tear down and a time to build,**
>
> **A time to weep and a time to laugh,**
>
> **A time to mourn and a time to dance,**
>
> **A time to scatter stones and a time to gather them,**
>
> **A time to embrace and a time to refrain,**
>
> **A time to search and a time to give up,**

A time to keep and a time to throw away,

A time to tear and a time to mend,

A time to be silent and a time to speak,

A time to love and a time to hate,

A time for war and a time for peace.

What does the worker gain from his toil? I have seen the burden God has laid on men. He has made everything beautiful in its time.

He has also set eternity in the hearts of men: yet they cannot fathom what God has done from beginning to end. I know that there is nothing better for men than to be happy and do good while they live.

That everyone may eat and drink, and find satisfaction in all his toil—this is the gift of God. I know that everything God does will endure forever; nothing can be added to it and nothing taken from it. God does it so that men will revere him.

So how does this relate to our writings in this book? It teaches us that **we only have a limited amount of time; we are born and we will die.** We must make use of our time in between to fully live, enjoy each other, teach others, do right, etc. We must pay attention so that we can act in an appropriate way towards all of the various situations in our lives. **So dive into life, laugh when you can, and be satisfied with having enough.** In the quote above, the beginning and the end are mentioned. We as humans cannot fully grasp what God has done from the beginning to the end. There are no easy answers. We must go on in faith and enjoy things while we have them and give thanks to God who gives us those good things. God has put everything in its place and time, so enjoy yourself. Make the best of every event in your life, whether it is joyful or sad, or somewhere in between. It is OK to have fun! Enjoy your home, your health, and your family. Enjoy activities such as cooking, hunting, playing sports, reading, etc. Everything has a purpose. It is your responsibility to react to it in a positive way, and learn what you can from the situation.

Society Contribution Issues

I don't remember how the subject came up or why we were discussing it, but I once asked my dad, "What have you contributed to society or the world to make it better?" He was not necessarily one to do a lot of community service, for example.

His response was, "I have succeeded in raising three children who are responsible, successful and are contributing to society in their own ways. None of them are a burden to the world. Also, I am not a burden, and have helped by raising a lot of food and paying taxes fairly." Needless to say there was great help from our mother, but at the moment the question was to him.

Even though there were times that I disagreed with his ways or philosophies, I still had to agree with him regarding the above statements and admire him for truly standing up for what he believed in.

How Much is Enough?

One of our grandfathers had a saying and it went like this: "The simple life is the best." Even though he died when I was very young, I remember him saying it more than once. He was born in the 1880's and lived to the age of 93. I believe that he enjoyed life very much even though he did not have a lot of what we would label today as necessities. Cell phones were not even dreamed of during his lifetime. I guess it relates to the saying "the good old days" before everything seemed to get so complicated. I don't think my grandfather ever believed that having a lot of money would make him any happier than he already was. He had his bills paid, owned some property, and had some savings in the bank. But he was content, something that not everyone (maybe most) can say about himself or herself today.

What did he do? Aside from his occupation of being a farmer/rancher, he and my grandmother certainly filled their free time. They played music, wrote songs, wrote poetry, were very well read, went to community events, played games, and had many more hobbies, including gardening, sewing, cooking, etc. Sure, there were rough times, the winters were still cold, there were some health issues, but when the day was done, they "blew out the coal-oil light" and retired to a good night's sleep. Was that really bad? No. Are we as individuals and as a society any happier today? We think probably not.

A large income or bank account will not guarantee happiness. In general, the more you have the more you want. Think about it. We will wager that at one time (maybe when you were in high school) just having a car, any car, would have made you happy. It signified some sort of freedom. But as your life progressed, you tended to want a better, bigger, faster, more fully optioned ride. Leather seats were needed to make you happy, and they did, at least temporarily. This goes back to needs vs. wants. Americans tend to always have more wants, regardless of the money resources they may currently have. **Having things is fine, as long as you can truly afford them and don't put them first in your life. You must find a balance in your life before you will be happy with what you have financially.**

You will find yourself never having enough money until you find a way to let go of all the material cravings that you have. People seem to be very driven to buy the latest cars, clothes, a fancier house, and more exotic vacations. How do people afford all of this? They continue working and in some cases go further and further into debt. It is good to be able to work, but the debt thing needs to be controlled. People are tending to work longer and harder hours, and seeing their stress levels continually rise just to keep up with their wants. Yes, wants. Not true needs. Such cravings have probably been part of human existence since the beginning. Once the basic needs are met, we still want more. We look around and see friends, neighbors, celebrities, and sometimes even people in other countries having more than we do. And we relate success with having a lot of money (and the things it affords). **But we can never be happy with what we have until we decide for ourselves to be content with what we have.**

That is not to say that you should get to a certain point and then stop trying to do anything else. Keeping that job, doing volunteer work, having a purpose in life will surely contribute to contentment also. You just may have to adjust your desires to be realistic on how much "stuff" you really need.

We've all heard "you can't take it with you" or as a friend says, "I've never seen a hearse with a luggage rack." Once the basic expenses for living (including taxes), funds for emergencies, and charitable contributions are met, how much more is needed? Really, the answer is none. But, it is OK and recommended to have a few luxuries to make life much more fun and enjoyable. The trick is to realistically decide for yourself just how much you need to

THE WINNING TRIUMPH

be content with. Each person, including you, plays the game of life differently. So how do you get the feeling of, "I'm the richest person in the world"? Simple: don't compare yourself to anyone else. Do what is best for you and makes you thrive. Enjoy your relationships, your family, your health, your faith, etc. And don't take them for granted.

CONSIDER THE POINTS BELOW WHEN DECIDING FOR YOURSELF HOW MUCH IS ENOUGH:

1) **What is it that truly makes you happy?** Knowing what this is will help you in your quest. For example, is it material things, people and/or activities? Remember our concept of **FAITH, FITNESS, FAMILY** and **FRIENDS**.

2) **Surviving financially in the world is one thing, thriving and having a vibrant life is another.** You must have enough to enjoy the things you want to do. You are the one that determines that level.

3) **Do you really need all of the "stuff" that you have accumulated?** Sometimes, it becomes more of a burden than a pleasure to you in ways such as keeping it clean, insured, safe from theft, maintained, etc.

4) **Why do you desire more and more?** To keep up with the neighbors maybe? Can you give up certain things or more things to simplify your life?

5) **If you didn't want so much more, could you not work as long and hard?** Remember, you are selling your time (and sometimes health) to gain more goods. Is it worth it?

6) **Remember that there are probably a lot of people living comfortably on a lower income than you have.**

Conclusion

Ultimately, the goal is for each of us to win the game. This is accomplished by accumulating sufficient assets and resources throughout our earning years to be able to yield a big enough return on those assets to afford the lifestyle you wish to live for as long as you have to. Quite a challenge, isn't it. This is a backwards equation because you determine the lifestyle. However, the pitfall that most fall into is that they let insufficient accumulations of these assets determine their lifestyle, and therefore, are disappointed with the outcome. Conversely there are those who amass overwhelming amounts of assets and material possessions yet do not win the game simply because they are not content or happy with the result.

Refer back to the **FUNDAMENTALS**. It is your responsibility. You can and must make the choices to direct the outcome.

Several years ago (and an economic cycle or two ago) I had a conversation with a friend. It was during a time of economic downturn. He seemed to be doom and gloom about the markets, etc. This person was in his early thirties at the time, and was worried about some balances in retirement funds being in reverse at the moment.

My quick response to him was a series of questions (*and his responses*) as follows:

1) **Are your children hungry?** *No.*
2) **Do you still have your job?** *Yes.*
3) **Do you need to take money from your savings today?** *No.*
4) **Are you retiring soon?** *No.*
5) **What is your age?** *32.*
6) **Have you heard of market and economic cycles?** *Yes.*

THE WINNING TRIUMPH

7) **Do you truly believe the economy/market will ALWAYS be going down?** *No.*

8) **Then why are you fretting so much over it?** *I guess I'm not so much now.*

He continues to invest, save for college for his children, spend some, and is still enjoying life. **In summary, don't make downs of the market all consuming and worrisome to you.**

True, there are some unknowns, health, economy and ultimately death. However, there are the choices each of us make on a daily basis to be prepared to face the challenges before us. Keep in the forefront of your mind the fact that you are never alone. There is your faith, family and friends, as well as being as healthy as you are, to carry you to great heights in this world. Good luck. God bless. We wish you great success in your "Game of Wealth."

INDEX